MARPA
Tibetan Translator Mystic

MARPA
Tibetan Translator Mystic

Jungney Lhamo

Heritage Classics

HERITAGE PUBLISHERS
19-A, Ansari Road, Daryaganj, New Delhi - 110002
Tel: 23266258, 23264444
Fax: 23263050, E-mail: heritage@nda.vsnl.net.in

ISBN: 978-81-70262-63-3

Design & layout
SPB Enterprises Pvt. Ltd.
www.spbenterprises.net.in

Jungney Lhamo (Jungney means source or origin and Lhamo means goddess) is the Tibetan name of *Sunita Pant Bansal*, a native of the Himalayan region, who has been studying and writing on Buddhist heritage, for nearly three decades. Some of her bestsellers are: *The Eternal Himalayas, On the Footsteps of Buddha* and *Milarepa: The Tibetan Poet-Mystic & His Songs*.

Printed in India

Preface

Tibetans carried the whole of Indian Buddhism directly from India to Tibet. Although early visitors to Tibet used the term "Lamaism" for Buddhism in Tibet, some scholars later criticized this term, as it suggests that Tibetans had invented a new Buddhism. They pointed out that Tibet had preserved the long tradition of Indian Buddhism in its entirety, and in that sense had not invented anything new. Tibetans preserved Buddhist teachings that had been handed down from the Buddha to Nagarjuna and Asanga up to Atisha, and then reached Tibet through various acharyas, masters, translators and Tibetan lamas. The most prominent master-translator among them was Marpa.

Although they kept this legacy of authentic Indian Buddhist teachings intact, Tibetans made a very significant contribution by developing Buddhism further. As a result, Tibetan Buddhism and Indian Buddhism are not identical. One key Tibetan contribution centres on the division of the Mahayana Buddhist teachings they had imported into *sutrayana* and *mantrayana*. There is no Tibetan equivalent for *tantrayana*; the term used in classical texts is mantrayana or *vajrayana*. The terms *sutra* and *tantra* are used to refer to two sections of the classical canon.

The sutra path of the teachings begins with the training in turning one's mind away from all worldly affairs and continues up through generating *bodhicitta*, or the mind of enlightenment, and training in the wisdom that sees ultimate reality. It encompasses the whole range of Buddha's teachings. This is not different from "Indian Buddhism."

The mantra path, or tantric teaching, is the second part of the teaching. It begins with receiving a tantric initiation, *abhisheka*, as this is the doorway to the vajrayana path. From that initiation one must proceed up to the highest point of attainment—union or integration (*yuganaddha*)—through the "generation stage" and the "completion stage". Thus, after receiving initiation one practises the appropriate *sadhana* or deity yoga. There are a whole range of practices that comprise the "generation stage", such as visualizing oneself as the deity and visualizing the whole atmosphere or environment as pure and divine in nature. The "completion stage" involves meditating upon the inner, subtle constituents of one's body, i.e. the channels, the winds (energy flowing through the channels), and the drops (particular substances flowing with that energy). These aspects comprise much more detailed and precise practices. These tantric teachings are also not different from "Indian Buddhism."

How then does Tibetan Buddhism differ from Indian Buddhism? Tibet's greatest contribution is the systematic combination of these two streams of Indian Buddhist teachings, sutra and tantra. Very often academic scholars say, "The Tibetans were great systematizers," meaning that Tibetans were very good at arranging various teachings and structuring them in a systematic presentation. Perhaps sometimes they overdid it. However, Tibetan masters were unique in developing a very systematic combination of these two streams.

It is not that when talking about tantra Indian Buddhist acharyas completely ignored sutra. Sutra teachings were present in the background. Again, when they presented sutra teachings, tantric teachings were implied. In the Tibetan tradition, however, sutra and tantra are more explicitly distinguished in texts. When lamas teach they emphasize the importance of their combination. This is referred to as: *mdo sngags zung 'brel*, or the "union of sutra and mantra." All the traditions—Sakya, Gelug, Kargyu, Nyingma—basically teach the combination of the sutra and tantra teachings.

Whereas in the Indian tradition there are not many texts which emphasize the combination of these two, in the Tibetan tradition it is emphasized in every text. Tsongkhapa's the *Great Treatise on the Stages of the Path (Lam Rim Chen Mo)*, for instance, is basically a sutra teaching. Over 99% is devoted to the sutra teachings. At the end, however, Tsongkhapa mentions how to train specifically in the vajrayana. Here Tsongkhapa devotes a few lines to explaining that this is not all, finally you must enter the mantra path. This is one good example of the combination. In fact, you will find very few Tibetan texts which do *not* exemplify this combination. If you look at any of the teachings of Marpa, you will find it is basically mantrayana in nature, but the presence of sutrayana teachings is evident.

Another key contribution of Tibetan Buddhism is the development of the teachings on the guru-disciple relationship. The guru-disciple relationship is an important subject in Indian Buddhism and also in all the traditions of Tibetan Buddhism. In Tibetan it is called *shay* nyen ten tsùl (bshes gnyen bsten tshul), a difficult term to translate. Literally this means "attending to the guru," and this phrase indicates that a disciple definitely needs a teacher.

The central place Tibetans give to teachings on the guru-disciple relationship is illustrated by the layout of the *Great Treatise on the Stages of the Path to Enlightenment (Lam rim chen mo)*. There are only two divisions: after the preliminaries it first discusses, "How to attend to a spiritual master," and then, "How to actually engage in the practice." This two-fold division is like the practice of putting two loads on a horse in the olden days: on one side is the guru-disciple relationship and on the other all the rest. They both have equal weight. Inspirational examples of this relationship that are often cited in all the traditions of Tibetan Buddhism are those of Marpa with his guru Naropa, Naropa with Tilopa, and Milarepa with Marpa. When I was a novice student at Drepung Monastery, the biggest Gelukpa monastery in Tibet, during the New Year vacations it was customary for a senior monk to read out Milarepa's biography to the others every evening, to inspire them towards guru-devotion and austerity.

Tibetan lamas are sometimes shy about discussing the guru-disciple relationship because they think it may look as if the first emphasis is on the guru or the speaker himself. The teachings on the guru-disciple relationship, however, are emphasized in scriptures and commentaries, and the tradition of following that practice is very much a living tradition, so we cannot pretend it is not there. What is important is to understand the main purpose of this emphasis on the guru-disciple relationship.

The scriptures emphasize first the qualities of the guru, the spiritual teacher. The requisite qualities of a qualified spiritual teacher are many, and different qualities are listed for different contexts. One oft-quoted list is from the *Mahayanasutralankara*. This text lists ten qualities of the spiritual teacher of Mahayana teachings. The Tibetan Kadampa Geshe Potowa says that five of these ten qualities are especially important. They sound very simple: the teacher should be, first, one whose mind has been tamed, second, one who is serene, and third, one who is thoroughly peaceful. These three qualities correspond to the three main trainings of Buddhism: ethical training (*sila*), meditation (*samadhi*), and wisdom (*prajna*). As these three aspects constitute the main body of the teaching of Buddhism, the teacher should be well trained in these. The fourth quality is compassion, because if that is lacking none of his or her other good qualities will be helpful. The fifth is that he or she should have the special quality of higher insight into ultimate reality. So these are the key qualifications of the teacher.

What the Tibetans did within this traditional guru-disciple relationship is to add another dimension by emphasizing guru yoga. Guru yoga means to see the guru as a deity. The sutrayana texts say that you should regard your guru as equal to a Buddha, because he or she is your direct link to Buddha. But they do not ask you to imagine your guru in the form of Buddha. This is the concept, but how should it be practised? One may sometimes have a problem understanding how to do this. In the mantrayana tradition you visualize your guru as a chosen deity. If you are the practitioner of a particular *sadhana* or ritual for a particular deity, you visualize your guru as that deity. So you worship the deity who is inseparable from your guru, but you do *not* worship your guru as a human being. It is more practicable this way, since to worship someone as human being may sometimes bring difficulties.

Though we know the qualities of the guru, how can you find out whether a guru has these qualities, especially in today's society? You can search for almost everything on a computer now, but you cannot find out whether a particular person is a genuine guru or a self-seeking guru. As there is a big wave of interest across the world in spiritual systems, in Buddhism, and in Tibetan Buddhism in particular, it is hard to know who is a genuine guru. Moreover, the Buddhist texts say that the gift of dharma is the supreme gift, but in today's context we can say the business of dharma sometimes seems to be the supreme business. There are so many so-called gurus seeking promotion of themselves as gurus. Because of this trend, one needs to be extra careful in the beginning. When one practises guru yoga the relationship should be more like the relationship one has with one's chosen deity. The Tibetan word for "chosen deity" is *yidam* which means "one that is kept in one's mind".

Furthermore, when attending a dharma talk by a spiritual teacher, one needs to consider one's intention. Just having listened to a spiritual talk you don't have to consider the speaker your guru. Choosing a guru is like choosing a doctor. If you have a serious illness you don't go to just any door with the label, "Doctor So-and-so," or "Expert/specialist So-and-so." You have to find out the qualifications of that doctor and also how you feel about her or him. Once you have decided to depend on that doctor, you follow that doctor's prescriptions. Buddhism is taught in that way. The dharma or teachings are like medicine; the Buddha, here represented by one's spiritual master, is like the doctor; and the sangha, spiritual community, acts like the helpers or nurses in the hospital.

In the context of Tibetan Buddhism, most of the biographical literature concerns ascetics, scholars or monks, but Marpa has the distinction of being a householder who led a normal life while at the same time making a tremendous contribution to developing Tibetan Buddhism through translation, and by training such illustrious disciples as Milarepa.

In the last half century or so, much literature on Tibetan Buddhism has become available in English and other languages. Many of these are translations, which require the reader to have a certain degree of background knowledge. The importance of the present book is that it is accessible to anybody irrespective of their familiarity with Tibetan Buddhism. Its publication will contribute to the proper understanding of Tibetan Buddhism.

Lama Doboom Tulku
Director
TIBET HOUSE
CULTURAL CENTRE OF H. H. THE DALAI LAMA
1, Institutional Area, Lodhi Road
New Delhi - 110003

Marpa
(1012-1097)

Marpa Lotsawa (1012-1097), sometimes known as Lhodak Marpa Chokyi Lodro or commonly as Marpa the Translator was a Tibetan Buddhist teacher credited with the transmission of many Buddhist teachings to Tibet from India, including the teachings and lineages of Vajrayana and Mahamudra.

Marpa enthusiastically sought Buddhist instruction in India. Although he eventually became a highly accomplished Buddhist master, Marpa neither founded nor joined a Buddhist institution, choosing instead to remain a married householder, landowner and businessman.

Born in Lhodrak Chukhyer in the southern part of Tibet, to an affluent family, Marpa began studying at a young age but was wild and untamed compared to other children. Marpa first received instruction for three years at Mangkhar with Drokmi Shakya Yeshe and mastered Sanskrit. He decided to travel to India to study with renowned Indian Buddhist masters. Marpa returned home to Lhodrak and converted his entire inheritance into gold to fund his travel expenses and to make offerings to teachers.

Marpa journeyed first to Nepal where he studied with Paindapa and Chitherpa, two famous students of Naropa. Paindapa later accompanied Marpa to Pullahari, near Nalanda University, where Naropa taught. Marpa spent twelve years studying with Naropa and other great Indian gurus. After twelve years he set forth on his journey back to Tibet to teach and continue his dharma activities.

Marpa travelled to India twice more and Nepal three more times and studied with Naropa and other great teachers including Maitripa. On his third visit to India, Naropa, who was engaged in tantric practices, proved difficult to find. However, eventually Marpa found him and received the final teachings and instructions from Naropa. It was then that Naropa prophesied that family lineage would not continue for Marpa, but that his lineage would be carried on by his disciples. Marpa now had received the full transmission, so Naropa formally declared Marpa to be his successor although he had other major disciples including Paindapa, Chitherpa, Sri Santibhadra or Kukuripa, and Maitripa.

Upon his return to Tibet, Marpa spent many years translating Buddhist scriptures and made a major contribution to the transmission of the complete Buddha-dharma to Tibet. Marpa continued to practice and give teachings and transmissions to many students in Tibet. After his third visit to India Milarepa became his disciple, who inherited his lineage in full. Marpa lived with his wife Dagmema and their sons in Lhodrak in the southern part of Tibet.

Contents

Contents

Early Years

Marpa was born Tarma Wangchuk in 1012 to Wangchuk Oser and Gyamo Sa Dode in Pesar in Trowo valley in the district of Lhodrak in Southern Tibet. He was one of the four children of his parents and his family was wealthy as they had fields and dairy farms.

From an early age, Marpa displayed a sense of stubbornness and was extremely short tempered. This made his father apprehensive about Marpa's future. He felt that if his son followed the right path, whether that of Dharma or of worldly life, it would be beneficial to him and other people. However, if he chose the path of destruction, it would be disastrous not only for him but for everyone around him. He therefore decided to guide him to the path of Dharma from the very beginning.

When Marpa was twelve years old, his father sent him to Lugyepa, a local teacher, who gave him the name Chokyi Lodro, and Marpa entered into the path of Dharma. He studied reading and writing, and with the help of his razor sharp mind, he mastered both the faculties with ease. In fact, his sense of understanding was so great

Marpa was always ready for a fight.

that whatever was taught to him on a day, he was able to quickly assimilate and knew the subject by heart the next day!

However, as Marpa grew up he not only looked fearsome, but also was very aggressive by nature. He was always ready for a fight. His family was of the view that such an attitude could result in Marpa harming himself or other people. The villagers were frightened by his looks and avoided him. The only places he could visit were his teacher and just one friend he had in the village.

This made Marpa's father sad, and he thought it would be better if his son were sent away to another place, far away, to pursue his studies. Marpa agreed to become a student and asked his father for provisions, and they offered him two yak loads of paper, a measure of gold, a ladle made out of silver, teakwood, and a roll of heavy silk brocade. And of course, he was also given a horse.

Marpa moved to the Monastery of Ugu Valley in the Mangkhar region and joined the tutelage of Drogmi Lotsawa, the great translator. Marpa studied under him for three years and not only mastered the Tibetan language but also Sanskrit. However, Marpa felt no karmic connection with Drogmi. and felt that the time had come for awakening his good karmic connection with Indian gurus.

He decided to give his guru as many offerings as he could, so as to please him, and then collect his share of the inheritance from his parents and go to India to study Dharma. So, he gave whatever wealth he had, to Drogmi, and what remained were the horse and the saddle, which he carried to Taktse, North of

Lato and exchanged them for gold.

On his way, Marpa met the Prince of Lokya who was returning to Kyerphu from the Monastery of Shira, where a student had invited him to come and read the sutras. Marpa asked him if he could go along with him – to which not only the Prince of Lokya agreed but offered Marpa complete hospitality. Marpa was very impressed and realised that this Prince was someone who kept his spiritual commitments. He told him that he was on his way to India (via Nepal) to learn translation and requested him to remember him with kindness and receive him when he returned. The Prince told him that since he was too old, he might not be able to meet Marpa again, but his children would welcome him whenever he returned, and that he must return to Kyerphu. He also gifted him a measure of gold and woollen cloth.

Marpa then returned to his village for a short while, but soon decided to go in search of one of the most famous scholars and masters of meditation, Naropa, who was in India. He told his parents of his plans and requested them to hand over to him his share of the family wealth and property. His parents and relatives discouraged him and suggested that he stay on in Tibet and practise Dharma. Marpa reminded his father that he was the one who had wanted him to go far away to study under a guru; and India was very far away, where he would definitely find an enlightened guru. Ultimately his parents gave in, and Marpa was given his share of inheritance. Barring a house and fields, he exchanged everything for eighteen measures of gold to carry with him. He then left for India.

Marpa's First
Journey to India

On the way to India at Tsinesar in Upper Nyang, Marpa met Nyo of Kharak, the translator who was also going to India. He enquired about Marpa and his plans and when Marpa told him that he was going to India to study Dharma, Nyo told him that it could be possible only if he had a lot of gold.

"You need lots of gold without which studying Dharma will be like drinking water from an empty flask. I have plenty of gold, so you should join me as my servant, and together we will have lots of gold," Nyo suggested.

Marpa agreed and travelled with Nyo as his servant, and after a long and arduous journey, they reached Nepal.

One day they saw many people crowding on a mountainside and enquired what was going on. They were informed that Chitherpa and Paindapa, the two Nepalese disciples of Naropa were there and the lady devotees were performing a Ganacakra. They were suggested that since they were Tibetans, they could join the function and would get to eat and drink.

The very name of Naropa triggered off a connection with a former life and Marpa thought this was the perfect moment to initiate the action of meeting with the enlightened one. He and Nyo joined the celebrations where Chitherpa was giving a lecture on Guhyasamaja.

Seeing the audience, Chitherpa suggested to Paindapa that since the Tibetans were unlikely to have received abhisheka, they might violate their vows by lecturing to them. To which Paindapa said, "They won't understand Nepalese. Tibetans are like oxen."

This remark made Nyo angry, as he understood Nepalese. He became so angry that he stopped listening to the Dharma discourse and started reciting the mantras.

The next day Marpa again wanted to go for the feast and listen to the Dharma lectures, but Nyo declined, as he felt insulted on being compared to an ox. So, Marpa went alone and when Chitherpa asked him why his friend had not come with him, Marpa told him that his friend understood Nepalese and Paindapa's remark had upset him. Chitherpa however told him that he and Paindapa have no karmic connection, but he was happy that Marpa had come.

After receiving the oral instructions of Catuhpitha and the ejection of consciousness, and the permission-blessing of the Devi Vetali, Marpa told Paindapa that he knew very little Sanskrit and wanted to study translation further, but did not have much gold to offer. He offered them a measure of gold each.

Chitherpa and Paindapa suggested that Marpa should visit Pandit Lord Naropa, the only guru who could teach Dharma without demanding gold. They also offered to send him to Lord Naropa whom they described as the second Buddha. Marpa felt at ease in the presence of the two disciples of Lord Naropa and thought to himself, 'I must abandon hope and fear as to whether I live or die, and go to Naropa.'

As per the advice of the two gurus, Marpa stayed on for three years at Svayambhunath to get used to the heat, after which the two brother gurus wrote a letter of recommendation to Prajnasimha, one of Naropa's sramaneras, advising him to take Marpa to Naropa.

Marpa in India

Marpa then travelled to Nalanda (in present day Bihar) in India with Nyo. On reaching, Marpa asked Nyo if he too would like to receive teachings from the great Mahapandit, to which Nyo said that he had some reservations about Naropa. He admitted that while Naropa was a great Pandit, but he had gone to Tilopa and given up his scholarship and was now practising Kusulu meditation. Nyo also told Marpa to continue to be his attendant, so he could use the gold they were carrying together; else he would not part with his possessions. He said that there were many great Pandits in other parts of India and Marpa had the option of travelling with him. Marpa declined the offer and Nyo left without parting with any of his gold.

Marpa went on to meet Prajnasimha and gave him the letter. He was told that Naropa had gone to the Western part of India and would be returning soon. Till then Marpa could stay with him and his needs would be taken care of. However, he was informed that very soon, there would be a message from the great guru himself.

Sure enough, next day at dawn, an atsara arrived with a message from Lord Naropa for Prajnasimha, which said that he should bring the Buddhist from Tibet, who was staying with him, to Pullahari where he was staying. Prajnasimha accompanied Marpa to the Golden Mountain monastery of Pullahari where he was introduced to Naropa.

Marpa's dream was achieved and he offered full prostrations as also flowers made of gold.

Naropa responded:

In accordance with the guru's prophecy,
My son, the worthy vessel Marpa Lodro,
From the Northern Land of Snow,
Is welcome to assume the regency.

Marpa's heart was filled with joy.

Lord Naropa first gave him the abhisheka of Sri Hevajra and the second section of the Hevajra-tantra, and went on to teach him the Vajrapanjara and the Samputa.

A year later Marpa took a break and went to the city where he met Nyo, who asked him what he had studied. They compared their knowledge and it was found that Marpa knew Hevajra better than Nyo.

Nyo then told him that Tibetans were well versed in Hevajra anyway and that there was a superior Father Tantra called

Marpa offered prostrations to Naropa.

Guhyasamaja, which enabled the prana to flow through one's fingertips and enabled the person to hold Buddha in the palm of his hand.

This baffled Marpa and he returned to Naropa and told him about his meeting Nyo in the city and requested him to teach him Guhyasamaja. Naropa suggested to Marpa that he should proceed to the West, to the monastery of Laksetra, in the Vihara Puranacandra and request Pandit Jnanagarbha, a master of Tantra, who was an exponent of Svatantramadhyamaka and had attained Siddhi.

Marpa visited Laksetra and there his wish was fulfilled. Jnanagarbha gave him abhisheka and oral instructions of Guhyasamaja and also the ritual traditions of Kriya and Yoga tantras and the various yogic applications. This resulted in the complete realisation of the meaning of the secret mantra in him. Marpa was grateful to Naropa as he felt that it was due to his blessings that he had achieved what he desired.

A joyful Marpa offered guru Jnanagarbha this Mandala of Vajra song:

Lord, you are the equal of all the Buddhas;
I prostrate to the gurus.
Pure realm, Mahapandit Naropa
And glorious Jnanagarbha, I pay homage at your feet.
I was born in Lhodrak in Tibet through the power of karma.
My father and mother raised me.
This one known as Marpa Lodro

Has been established in the Dharma through their kindness.
To my father and mother, I prostrate with devotion.
Grant your blessings so that their kindness can be repaid with the
Dharma.
On the mandala of unborn nature
I arrange the flowers of manifold phenomena.
I make offering to the body of the gurus.
Grant your blessings to my body.

On the mandala of completely pure space
I arrange the flowers of unceasing coincidence.
I make offering to the speech of the gurus.
Grant your blessings to my speech.

On the mandala of the mind of great bliss
I arrange the flowers of abruptly cut thoughts.
I make offering to the mind of the gurus.
Grant your blessings to my mind.

On the mandala of the jewelled ground
I arrange the flowers of Mount Meru and the four continents.
I make offering to the body, speech, and mind of the gurus.
Grant your blessings to my body, speech, and mind.

On the universal ground of the pure realm,
From the five elements arise
Drinking water, flowers, incense,
Light, perfumed water, food, music, and other such offering
substances.

Whatever is excellent
I offer to the lord gurus.
Grant your blessings so that I may be free from obstacles.

As limitless as space,
Parasols, victory banners, music,
Canopies, drapery, and the like
Emanate from my mind and I offer them.
Grant your blessings so that my realisation may increase.

From the Buddha Jnanagarbha
I listened to the great tantra, the Guhyasamaja.
I understood it as the union of upaya and prajna.
I understood it as the key of Dharma.
I understood it as the ocean of tantra.
I received both material gifts and the Dharma.
The tree of my heart was made to grow
And the leaves of spotless Dharma words flourished.
Possessing the five wisdoms,
I benefit all beings.
It is pleasant to travel the supreme path of the five stages.
Luminosity, illusory body, and dream —
All these precious oral instructions you have given to me.
Jnanagarbha, you are so kind.
From now until the culmination
Of unsurpassable enlightenment is attained,
Please adorn the top of my head as the crown jewel of great
bliss.
You are never separate from the center of my heart.

Free from sadness and fear, I take refuge in you.
Holding the radiant hook of compassion,
Please clear away the darkness of ignorance.
Please accept my body, speech, and mind.

Marpa then returned to Pullahari to meet Naropa and on the
way he met Nyo, who again wanted to know what he had learnt
since their last meeting. Marpa proudly told him that he had
learnt Father Tantra, to which Nyo again wanted to compare
their knowledge on the subject. And again Marpa proved to be
the superior one.

As in the previous meeting, Nyo told Marpa, that like the Father
Tantra there was also a Mother Tantra called Mahamaya, which
contained oral instructions on the stillness of the nadis, the
movement of prana and the placement of bodhicitta. Nyo also
told him that Guhyasamaja was already well known in Tibet.
Once again Marpa was at a loss and on meeting Lord Naropa
told him about Mahamaya.

Mahamaya, the Mother Tantra

Naropa first asked him if he had fully understood Guhyasamaja to which Marpa told him that he had received the teaching to his full satisfaction. Naropa surprised Marpa by telling him that he had sent Marpa to Jnanagarbha to learn Guhyasamaja, since the time was not appropriate to teach him personally, but that he would do so when the time came. Naropa told him that while he also knew Mahamaya, he would rather send Marpa to the master of Mother Tantra, Kukuripa, also known as Glorious Santibhadra, who could be found on an island in a poison lake.

Naropa then pointed in the direction of charnel ground and instantly, from the charnel ground of Sosadvipa arrived three yoginis. Naropa told them that he was sending his 'son' Marpa to the poison lake in the South and that all three of them should bless him so that he faced no obstacles.

One yogini offered to protect Marpa from the danger of poisonous snakes; another offered to protect him from ferocious animals and the third from evil spirits.

*The human figure sitting under a tree, covered
with feathers, was Kukuripa.*

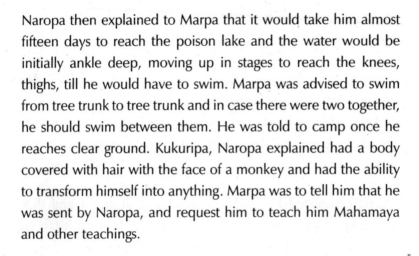

Naropa then explained to Marpa that it would take him almost fifteen days to reach the poison lake and the water would be initially ankle deep, moving up in stages to reach the knees, thighs, till he would have to swim. Marpa was advised to swim from tree trunk to tree trunk and in case there were two together, he should swim between them. He was told to camp once he reaches clear ground. Kukuripa, Naropa explained had a body covered with hair with the face of a monkey and had the ability to transform himself into anything. Marpa was to tell him that he was sent by Naropa, and request him to teach him Mahamaya and other teachings.

The trip to the poison lake in South India was difficult. The roads were difficult to follow. There were no animals, except the two birds he had seen flying ahead of him. On reaching the poison lake, lightning flashed, thunderbolt struck the ground and even though it was mid day, the sky became pitch black. The atmosphere was scary to say the least. Marpa remembered the promises made by the yoginis and yelled out the name of Mahapandit Naropa. The sky became clear.

Marpa then began his search for Kukuripa. He found a human figure sitting under a tree, covered with feathers of a bird! The man had tucked his face in the crook of his arm. Marpa asked him if he knew the whereabouts of Kukuripa and the man while ridiculing Marpa told him that he knew of no such man who lived there. Marpa searched elsewhere and then remembered his guru's words. He was now sure that the man he had met was Kukuripa himself! He went back to him and told him that

Mahapandit Naropa had sent him and that he wanted to learn the Mahamaya Tantra. Marpa then offered him gifts.

Kukuripa first jokingly mocked Naropa and then admitted that he was a very learned man. It was Naropa's sacred outlook that had made him send Marpa to Kukuripa, to learn the Mahamaya, though he knew it all himself as well. Thus, Kukuripa agreed to teach Marpa.

Marpa completed his studies without any obstacles and then arranged for a feast to express his gratitude to his guru. With joy in his heart he asked for permission to offer this song:

Lord, heart son of all the buddhas,
Vajradhara for all beings,
Holder of the treasury of the secret tantras,
Glorious Santibhadra, I pay homage at your feet.
Seeing your body crumbles my mountain of pride.
Hearing your speech frees my being from petty mind.
Remembering your mind dispels outer and inner darkness.
These days I am fortunate.

I came to the land of India from Tibet.
I am a man who has travelled a long way.
I requested the holy Dharma from pandits.
I received the holy Dharma of the direct lineage.
I touched the feet of the lord who possesses siddhi.

Having pacified obstacles of humans and spirits,
I received the father and mother tantras of the secret mantra.

I am a teacher who has received the great oral instructions.
Glorious Santibhadra has accepted me.
I am the only son of the good guru.

Without obstacles I travelled South to Nepal.
I am a Buddhist of fortunate karma.
The king of tantras, Cakrasamvara, seems to be easy,
As this holy Dharma was accomplished in a short time.
Having heard an auspicious prophecy,
I realise the value of obtaining a human birth.
My umbilical cord was cut in Lhodrak in Tibet.
My fortunate karma was reawakened in India.
Meeting siddhas and pandits,
Receiving abhishekas, expositions of tantra, and oral instructions,
My body, speech, and mind were blessed.

At the feet of the lord of dakinis,
I learned the meaning of the three yogas
And met the mother Great Miracle.
Attending the father, All-Good,
I sharpened my experience of samadhi on the path of passion.
Brightening the lamp of the three kinds of prajna,
Dispelling the darkness of the three delusions,
Burning up the fuel of the three obscurations,
Emptying the graves of the three lower realms,
Oh, how very kind is the lord guru!
Oh, how happy is Chokyi Lodro!
Oh, how joyful to be with all the dharma brothers and sisters
here!

Marpa then thought that he must now return to Naropa.

In general, Marpa had indestructible faith in the famous Master Maitripa, and so continually thought, "I must by all means receive teachings from him." In particular, the night before a farewell ganacakra to be performed by the guru Kukuripa, Marpa vividly remembered the guru Maitripa again and again, and supreme faith was born in him. Mentally he offered a mandala and performed the sevenfold service; then he supplicated Maitripa.

In a dream that night, a beautiful maiden holding a vase in her hand appeared, and said she was a messenger of Maitripa. She placed the vase on top of Marpa's head. When Marpa awoke, he experienced immeasurable joy.

The next day, as Jetsun Marpa was preparing to depart, glorious Santibhadra performed a farewell ganacakra for him and gave him scriptures of the teachings that he had bestowed upon him. He placed his hand on top of Marpa's head and said, "The path to this place is difficult to travel. By coming here you have received great benefit. Because he knew you were a worthy person, Naropa sent you to me. Now you will also be sent to Maitripa. Naropa himself has accepted you through his kindness. After he has given you whatever oral instructions you want, he will empower you as his regent to tame disciples in the Land of Snow. I knew you were coming beforehand, and sent two protectors transformed into men to escort you. You did not see them as men, but as birds. Now, having given you oral instructions and scriptures, I bestow on you the auspicious empowerment. Take delight in this." Thus Kukuripa was very pleased.

All this accorded with Marpa's dream and prophecy. He experienced irreversible faith in guru Kukuripa, and immeasurable great joy. As a parting gift, Marpa offered this song of realisation to the guru and the dharma brothers and sisters:

Jetsuns who reside here,
Heart friends, brothers and sisters, please listen.
I, stubborn Marpa the Translator,
Went South to Nepal when my karmic link was reawakened.
From the Nepalese who possess siddhi,
And from Jnanagarbha and Santibhadra,
I received the Catuhpitha, Guhyasamaja, and Cakrasamvara.
The treasury of tantras and oral instructions was opened.
Now, in the presence of the master, I requested and was given oral instructions
And received auspicious prophecies at the same time.
The other night,
I mentally arranged a mandala,
Supplicated Maitripa, and then fell asleep.
In the confused habitual patterns of dream,
A messenger of Master Maitripa,
A maiden of radiant beauty,
Arrived holding a vase in her hand.
I dreamt that she touched it to my head.
I thought, "This must be a blessing of Maitripa's kindness.
It is the result of former aspiration and a karmic link."
Therefore, with intense longing and faith,
I will go into the presence of the venerable father.

To you, the jetsun who resides here,
Unceasing devotion arises.
I take refuge so that we will be inseparable.
Grant your blessings so that the lower realms may cease to exist.

All you vajra brothers and sisters,
Friends with whom I am joined in this life and the next,
Cast behind you the deceptive seductions of samsara.
Practice the holy oral instructions.
Keep samaya free from hypocrisy.
Always meditate on the guru on the top of your head.
Enjoy the ten virtues.
Abandon the ten non-virtues like poison.
Practice continually without interruption.

Guru Santibhadra put his hand on top of Marpa's head, granting a blessing so that Marpa would be free from obstacles.

Now Marpa knew the aspects of the Mahamaya.

Naropa and Maitripa

In three days time Marpa reached Pullahari and briefed Naropa of his learnings from Kukuripa.

After some time, Marpa decided to meet Nyo who was then in Nalanda, learning under Guru Balimtapa. Again while comparing their knowledge on Mahamaya, Marpa emerged victorious. Nyo asked him who taught Marpa the Mother Tantra, to which Marpa replied:

My guru possesses the three yogas.
His form is inferior, but his mantra is profound.
He is a yogin of the ultimate Dharma,
Known as the One Who Shows the Path to Liberation.
At this moment, he is in the city of Kapilavastu.

But, he kept the name secret.

Nyo went to Kapilavastu, but could not find Kukuripa.

Marpa then sought the permission of Naropa to meet Maitripa

Marpa met Maitripa at the monastery of Blazing Fire Mountain.

and went to meet him at the monastery of Blazing Fire Mountain. On meeting the guru his heart was filled with joy and he offered this song:

In order to benefit beings in Jambudvipa,
You took birth in a royal family.
You know the variety of outer and inner sadhanas.
I prostrate to you, Maitripa.
Arya Tara gave you prophecies
And unobstructed blessings.
You touched the dust of Lord Savari's feet.
I praise you, Avadhuti.

Your body is a mountain of precious gold.
Your wisdom, aspiration, and the like are pure.
You quell the disease of the klesas.
I praise you, son of Dharma.

The sunyata vajra of your mind
Crumbles the great mountain ranges of belief in a self.
You see the quality of all Dharmas.
I praise you, unequalled lord guru.

Nirmanakaya, ornament of all Jambudvipa,
Essence of Vajrasattva,
Refuge of beings, possessing the treasure of kindness,
I praise you, crest ornament.

Amongst the hordes of humans, spirits, and demons,

All vicious ones without exception
Obey your command through the power of your yogic discipline.
I praise you, vajra holder.

Kind sugata gurus,
You gave up your subjects to act for the holy Dharma.
From Mahapandit Naropa and other gurus
I received instructions
And finished this study of the tantras.

At the mountain island in the boiling poison lake in the South,
While I was staying at the feet of glorious Santibhadra,
You, holy one, kindly accepted me.
Not concerned for my life, I came to see you.

At the monastery of the Blazing Fire Mountain,
In the cool shade of a nyagrodha tree,
Master, Prince Maitripa,
Father Buddha, now I meet you.

Faith arises like the sun
And I am so moved by faith that I even dare to die.
I supplicate without hypocrisy.
Please bless me continuously.

You hold the tradition of the Great Brahmin
And stayed with the emanation, Lord Savari.
Please give me the holy Dharma, well taught by them,
The essential meaning of the pinnacle of all yanas,

The mahamudra free from extremes,
Which is like space.

Maitripa accepted Marpa as his student and gave him the complete abhishekas and the oral instructions on the transmission of Mahamudra. When Marpa practised the teachings, he had excellent experiences and achieved great realisation.

At a ganacakra Marpa offered this song to describe his realisation and experience:

In the palace of great bliss on top of my head
On a spotless lotus, sun, and moon
Dwells the guru Master, the loving protector.
Please bless my mind.
All the buddhas of the three times
And the countless hosts of yidams and devas
Are inseparable from you, glorious Avadhuti.
Please remain on the lotus in my heart.
Grant me mastery over speech.

In the pure realm of India
Dwell Mahapandit Naropa and others.
The dust of the feet of those siddhas
I touched to the top of my head.

Listening to many words of the tantras
I was not satisfied even by these.
Therefore, I came to the jetsun Master

And properly requested the blessing of the holy Dharma.

In particular, I requested the mahamudra.
Doubts about the teachings I knew were cut.
Teachings that I did not know, I studied.
Blessings and realisation
In the tradition of Lord Saraha occurred at once. .

I sing a song offering my realisation to the lord.
All the various outer and inner schools
Are realised and unified in mahamudra.
All the limitless deceptive appearances
Arise as manifestation of the unity of equality.

This unceasing Dharma
Is unobstructed, self-luminous insight.
Within innate insight, unity,
Spontaneous wisdom is the view.

Throughout the four activities of postmeditation,
Inseparable in the three times, like a flowing river,
This yoga is lucid, free from obscurations.
Free from distraction is the meditation.

The dharmas of body, speech, and mind, and the three times
Are an unpredictable variety adorned with a single ornament —
Unceasing, effortless, and the same in essence.
Like an illusion is the action.

The essence of realisation is nowness,
Occurring all at once, with nothing to add or subtract.
Self-liberation, innate great bliss,
Free from hope or fear is the fruition.

Regardless of how many words one hears,
At last the ground of mind is understood as dharmakaya.
At last my doubts are exhausted.
At last the ground and root of confusion are destroyed.
I do not hope for enlightenment through sophistry.

Thus, in the presence of the great lord Master,
Through the fruition of practicing the essence
And through the blessings of the lineages,
I offer this understanding, experience, and realisation.

May the jetsun guru and dharma friends
Gathered here rejoice!

Master Maitripa then sang this vajra song of twelve instructions
to Marpa:

O son, if the root of faith is not firm,
The root of nonduality will not be firm.
If you do not develop unbiased compassion,
The two rupakayas will not be attained.
If the three paramitas are not practiced,
Realisation will not arise.

If you do not attend the jetsun guru,
The two siddhis will not be attained.
If you have not cut the root of mind,
Do not carelessly abandon awareness.
If you cannot strike phenomena with mudra,
You should not retreat into great bliss.
If thoughts of desire arise,
You should act like a joyful elephant.
If occasionally the klesas arise,
Look at the mind and meditate without distraction.
If the mind is harmed by unfavourable conditions,
Practice the four abhishekas continually.
If klesas arise in your being,
Remember the guru's instructions.
If you do not supplicate one-pointedly,
How can you fulfill the intentions of the holy ones?
If you do not meditate in the union of utpatti and sampannakrama,
How can you realise the inseparability of samsara and nirvana?
This is a vajra song of twelve instructions.
Remembering these makes thirteen.
If these yogas are practiced,
You will remain on the thirteenth bhumi.

Marpa was delighted with these instructions and assimilated them. He then returned to Naropa at Pullahari, who had further instructions for him.

Naropa said, "On the shores of the poison lake in the South, in the charnel grounds of Sosadvipa is Jnanadakini, adorned with bone ornaments. Whoever encounters her is liberated. Go before her and request the Catuhpitha. You can also request the Kusulus there for whatever teachings you desire."

So, in the charnel grounds at Sosadvipa, Marpa went and met the yogini, who was living in a grass hut. Offering her a mandala of gold, he supplicated before her. She joyfully gave him the full abhisheka and oral instructions of the Catuhpitha. Moreover, Marpa received abhishekas and oral instructions on Utpatti and Sampannakrama from kusulu yoginis. He also requested oral instructions for various practical uses. Thus, he became a treasury of oral instructions. Finally, Marpa returned to Naropa.

Naropa asked, "What realisations did the abhishekas and oral instructions arouse in you?" Marpa told him what had happened and Naropa was very pleased.

Marpa now supplicated before Naropa, saying, "I want the abhisheka of Cakrasamvara and instructions on the Commentary to the Tantra."

Naropa gave him the full abhisheka, as well as the instructions on the Commentary to the Tantra, and said, "Practising them is of great importance."

Marpa - Path to Realisation

Having been given the renowned oral instructions of the four special transmissions, the six yogas of Naropa, and the mahamudra transmission showing the mind as innate co-emergent wisdom, Marpa meditated.

Many special experiences and realisations of the unsurpassable secret mantra were born in Marpa's mind. He actualised the unity of bliss, luminosity, and non-thought. For seven days, he was unable to move the gates of body, speech, and mind, and he established confidence in this. The ten signs arose, and in a joyful state of mind, the days and nights passed.

Later, Marpa thought to himself, "I have spent about twelve years in Nepal and India. Not only have I received abhishekas and oral instructions, I have also studied and practised both their words and meanings. Therefore I have no regrets, and I do not have to emulate others. Now that my gold is almost spent, I should return to Tibet to obtain as much gold as I can. Then I will return to India and please my gurus by offering it to them. I will thoroughly review with them the teachings previously obtained, and I will obtain whatever I did not receive before. Now I must, by all means, spread the teachings of Buddha in Tibet, and the teachings of the Practice Lineage."

He then assembled the necessary provisions, using the remainder of his gold, and kept just enough for expenses on the road.

Marpa offered a ganacakra of thanksgiving and celebration to Mahapandit Naropa. At the feast, he thought to himself, "Fulfilling my purpose in coming to India from Tibet, I have met many gurus who are learned and who have attained siddhi. I have received and studied many tantras along with their commentaries. I have become the model of a learned translator who knows the languages. Pure experiences and realisations have arisen in my being. Now, as I am returning to Tibet without obstacles, there is no happier day than today."

Marpa then sang the first of eight grand songs to glorious Naropa. This is the song in which he offered his realisation:

Lord, authentic precious guru!
Because of the merit accumulated by your previous practice,
You met the nirmanakaya Tilopa in person.
The suffering of existence, which is difficult to abandon,
You scorned throughout your twelve trials.
Through your practice of austerities,
You saw the truth in an instant.
I prostrate at your feet, Sri Jnanasiddhi.
I, the translator, a novice from Tibet,
Through the karmic link of previous practice

Marpa offered a ganacakra of thanksgiving.

Met you, Mahapandit Naropa.
I studied the Hevajra-tantra, famed for its profundity.
You gave me the essence, Mahamaya.
I received the inner essence, Cakrasamvara.
In general, I extracted the inner essence of the four orders of
tantra.
As granted by the mother Subhagini,
Whose river of blessings is continuous,
You transmitted the four abhishekas to me.
I gave birth to undefiled samadhi
And established confidence in it in seven days.
The sun and moon, the life force and descent,
Were locked in the home of still space.
The experience of self-existing co-emergence—
Bliss, luminosity, and non-thought—dawned from my heart.
The confusion of habitual sleep
Was realised as the nature of the path of luminosity.
The movements of the mind, both grasping and fixation,
Dissolved into the simplicity of dharmakaya.
Outer appearance, this illusory contrivance,
Was realised as unborn mahamudra.
Inner fixation, this mind consciousness,
Like meeting an old friend,
Realised its own nature.
Like a dream dreamt by a mute,
An inexpressible experience arose.
Like the ecstasy experienced by a maiden,
An indescribable meaning was realised.
Lord Naropa, you are very kind.

Previously, you gave me blessings and abhishekas;
Please continue to accept me with your kindness.

Mahapandit Naropa placed his hand on top of Marpa's head, and sang this song of blessing:

You, Marpa the Translator from Tibet!
Do not make the eight worldly dharmas the goal of your life.
Do not create the bias of self and other, grasping and fixation.
Do not slander friends or enemies.
Do not distort the ways of others.
Learning and contemplating are the torch that illumines the darkness.
Do not be ambushed on the supreme path of liberation.
Previously, we have been guru and disciple;
Keep this with you in the future; do not give this up.
This precious jewel of your mind,
Do not throw it in the river like an idiot.
Guard it carefully with undistracted attention,
And you will accomplish all needs, desires, and intentions.

Hearing this, Marpa greatly rejoiced and made a vow that he would return again, and then left for Tibet.

On the Way to Tibet

While on the long and tedious journey back to Tibet, Marpa and his fellow traveller Nyo had to face a lot of difficulties. Both Marpa and Nyo had met each other as they had planned earlier and had started to make the journey back to Tibet together. As they trudged along the rough hilly terrain that they had to cover, both travellers realised that they were running out of the provisions, which they were carrying with them. And during these pangs of desperations, Nyo's mind started working in a rather different way.

Nyo started to think that though he was the one who carried more gold with him, Marpa turned out to be more learned of the two. This thought kept nagging him from within. As it was, their route back home was troublesome, and on top of that, these evil thoughts wore Nyo down even more. His mind started to formulate a plan.

Nyo had brought with him two of his pandit friends, an atsara and some other people who were basically brought along to carry his books and his other baggage. Marpa, on the other hand was

The atsara threw Marpa's books into the river.

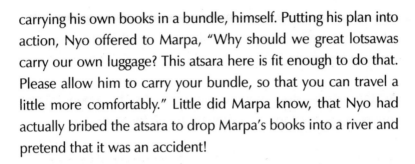

carrying his own books in a bundle, himself. Putting his plan into action, Nyo offered to Marpa, "Why should we great lotsawas carry our own luggage? This atsara here is fit enough to do that. Please allow him to carry your bundle, so that you can travel a little more comfortably." Little did Marpa know, that Nyo had actually bribed the atsara to drop Marpa's books into a river and pretend that it was an accident!

So when they were crossing the Ganges, the atsara, on Nyo's orders, threw Marpa's bag into the river, pretending that he had tripped on a stone – and with it went all the books that Marpa had been carrying in it. Marpa knew that this was no accident and that the fact was that it was Nyo who had instructed the atsara to do the same. He first pondered to himself, "It is definitely easy to find gold in Tibet, but it is nearly impossible to look for gurus in India. These teachings and oral instructions that I had, were more important than all the gold that could be found anywhere in the world. Should I too then jump into the water?"

But though he kept thinking about it for a long time, he remembered all that his guru had taught him and he was successful in calming down his mind after a while. Though Marpa was not looking for revenge, he still decided to tell Nyo that he knew about the whole plan and he knew that it was Nyo who was responsible for the loss of his books. "I didn't do it," was all that Nyo had to say in return.

As soon as the boat reached the shore, Marpa grabbed the atsara and declared that he would take the matter before the king and only then would he be happy that justice had been dealt. But the very mention of the king's name made the atsara blurt out the whole story before Marpa. He told him everything that Nyo had ordered him to do.

As the whole story now came out into the open, Marpa immediately burst into this song of shame for Nyo:

Listen to me, companion met through the power of karma.
You are the man I agreed to travel with.
In general, you have entered the gate of Dharma.
In particular, you are known as a lotsawa, pandit, and guru.
With perverted intentions you entered the boat.
Even though you cannot benefit someone,
In general, you should not cause harm to another.
In particular, by harming the teachings of Buddha,
You have injured me and all sentient beings.
How could you possibly cause such harm?

By the thought and deed of the five poisonous klesas,
Along with my books
You threw the fame you cultivated,
Your gold, and the holy Dharma into the water.
It is not the material value I am thinking of,
But these special teachings were precious for others.
I am sad that others will not be benefited.

However, by my earnest application and questioning,
The Dharma and my mind have mixed.
I clearly recall their words and meaning.

Returning to India again,
I need only ask for them
From Mahapandit Naropa and other siddha gurus.

Today, you should abandon
The name of guru, dharma teacher, and lotsawa.
With remorse and repentance, return to your country.
Confess your evil deeds and do rigorous penance.
Thinking and acting as you have done
And boasting that you are a guru,
Though you might deceive a few fools,
How can you ripen and free those who are worthy?
With your precious human body so difficult to gain,
Please do not cultivate the three lower realms.

Marpa then concluded what he had to say to Nyo.

Extremely ashamed at his actions, Nyo pleaded, "Please do not worry. I will let you copy everything from the original texts that I have with me." But Marpa adamantly pointed out that their gurus and oral instructors were different. So even if Nyo did lend him his books they would be of no use to him.

"I would rather focus on what I have left in my mind," was what Marpa said.

Marpa had started to wonder whether he should return to India and start his learning all over again, but then he turned to Nyo once again and said, "Do lend me those books later."

Once they reached Nepal, Marpa had another thought in his mind. He decided that travelling with Nyo would only make him achieve more bad thoughts and misdeeds. He therefore turned to his companion and informed him that he would like to travel to Tibet on his own from thereon. Nyo begged him not to mention the incident of the loss of his books to anyone and said, "Just come to my house and I will lend you the books as I have promised." Marpa assured him that he would not breathe a word about their little tiff and went off on his own.

Parting of Ways

Nyo travelled with his entourage from there to the Nepal-Tibet border. From there he sent a message to his attendants that they should meet him there. When they arrived, Nyo left for Kharak along with them.

On the road, Marpa met guru Chitherpa. The guru was also travelling along with his dharma friends, headed by his friend White Hadu. When they saw Marpa they gave him a grand reception and welcomed him warmly. As they settled down, Chitherpa and his friends turned to Marpa and praised the fact that he had been calm when the evil Nyo had thrown his books into the water. They also appreciated the fact that he had sung him a song to show him the error of his ways. "You have been able to control your anger through your meditation practice and we are now confident that you have mastered it well. Now that you have lost all your texts, we would like you to sing us a song from your own mind about the ultimate view."

Heeding to the request made by the noble men before him, Marpa sang:

O holy guru who is the guide,
And you who are headed by White Hadu
And who have completed your study of the sutras and tantras,
Listen for a moment to a Tibetan's song.
The ultimate view is very special,
Indivisible and non-dwelling.
It is the mind of the victorious ones of the three times.
Those who want to separate upaya and prajna
Must be prevented from falling into extremes.

To speak to such learned ones as you is difficult.
I have not sung this song before, so it may not go well.
Nonetheless, listen and I will sing you a song of the sastras.

Preventing the grasping onto things as real
Is said to be the only way to conquer the hordes of Mara.
Understand that grasping in this way causes obscuration.
As for the glory of servants and personal virtues,
Abandon special attempts to gain it.

Ignorant ones believe that "emptiness" is nihilism.
The extreme of nihilism undermines the accumulation of virtue.
Those who desire flowers in the sky
Destroy the harvest of virtue
With the hail of perverted views.

One should know the characteristics of space.
All those who do not know emptiness
Claim non-existence is existence.

The perverted regard a mirage as water.
Ignorance about the truth is the cause of samsara.
Cittamatrins and heretics like the Sankhyas and the rest
Maintain that upaya and prajna are separate.
Each has his own theory.
This is the same as maintaining that a dead tree has flowers.

Free from all assumptions
Is non-dwelling truth.
Knowing this fully is prajnaparamita.
Not dwelling in the extremes of samsara and nirvana,
Compassion possesses the essence of emptiness
And unifies upaya and prajna.
This is self-existing co-emergence.
In the same way, I understand
Bliss-emptiness and insight-emptiness
As not being different.

Non-conceptual compassion
And the primordial nature of emptiness
Are inseparable in the nature of simplicity.
You should understand all dharmas like this.

As for the view that is merely shown by words,
See this as an object of clinging.
In accord with the common view,
Have confidence in the cause and result of karma.
It does not wear out in a hundred kalpas,
Just as the supreme wise one has said.

People without compassion
Are like sesame seeds burnt by fire.
How could further seeds come from that?
If there is no ground, how could there be any characteristics?
Therefore, these people cannot enter the mahayana.
Thus said the supremely wise Nagarjuna.

If there is not a proper view of the objects of mind,
It is useless to give the holy Dharma.
It is like chaff with no grain.
Thus says Marpa Lotsawa.

You whose minds are vast with the truth of wisdom,
If I have the wrong meaning, please forgive me.

Chitherpa and his friends, as also White Hadu, were overjoyed
to hear what Marpa had to say.

Marpa's Dream

Marpa was still on his way to Tibet, when he came to a village that lay very close to the Nepal-Tibet border, called Lisokara. The officers at Lisokara were renowned for collecting many custom taxes. It so turned out that Lord Marpa had to stay at that village for many days after arriving.

One night, when Marpa lay asleep, he had a very strange dream. He dreamt that he was being lifted in a palanquin by dakinis and they carried him all the way to Sri Parvata. There, Marpa met the great Brahmin Saraha. He dreamt that Saraha was overjoyed to see Marpa and consequently blessed his body, speech and mind. And as if that were not enough, Saraha also gave to Marpa the signs of the essential truth, Mahamudra. As these signs became clear to him, Marpa felt an eternal bliss dawn on his body and mind. That night, as Marpa slept on, he was filled with immeasurable delight. Much later, after Marpa awoke and started with his daily activities, Saraha's words rung sharply in his ears. It was in that happy state that Marpa left for Langpokhar, which was situated in the province of Mang. He lived there for nearly two months,

Marpa dreamt of a woman, who told him how to pray to Sri Parvata.

teaching Dharma.

Meanwhile, there was a new development in Tsang at Kyerphu. The Prince of the region, Lokya had passed away. His eldest son was now named the new Prince. On ascending the throne, the Prince was informed that Marpa was staying close by, in a place called Kyitrong. Hearing this, the Prince immediately dispatched a messenger to go to Marpa and invite him to Kyerphu.

Marpa warmly accepted. As he reached Kyerphu, he received a grand reception. Marpa stayed on there for a month and taught the people there about Dharma. Soon, on the tenth day of the waxing moon, during the festival of dakas, a ganacakra was held. There, during the festivities, the Prince turned to Marpa and reminded him how he had joined his father in welcoming Marpa the last time he had come to Kyerphu. "Guru, may I request you during this grand and auspicious day, to sing a song for us, a song that you have not sung before, a song that will unify words and meaning?" he requested.

Marpa replied, "Last spring, I was at a place very near from here, a place called Lisokara. During my long stay there, I had a dream one night. I saw a woman come to me, dressed as a Brahmin's daughter and told me how we should pray to Sri Parvata. I was only too glad to accompany this lady because I could feel that she was no ordinary being. Once I reached the blessed place, I met the great Brahmin there myself. It was there that I heard the song of essential truth and none other than the great Brahmin himself sang it to me. I will sing that song for you now."

And so saying, Marpa sang his song:

On this glorious and auspicious day of the waxing moon,
The holiday of the tenth day,
At the ganacakra feast of the dakas,
A son who is unswerving in samaya,
You, the prince of Lokya, have requested, "Sing a song never heard before."
I have travelled a long way on the road,
And my body is overcome with weariness.
Therefore, this song will not be melodious nor ravishing to your mind,
And I am not even skilled in composing songs.
But because there is no one more important than you, my friend,
And since I cannot refuse an important man,
I will sing a wondrous song which has never been heard before,
A song of the sayings and thoughts of the Lord Brahmin
You, the many monks and tamrikas who fill these seats,
Listen carefully and consider this in your hearts.

In the third month of last spring,
I came up from the land of central Nepal.
After being on the road the time of one meal,
I arrived at the Nepalese custom-tax station
In a town of lower caste people.
The custom-tax collectors exploit any man they meet,
And detain defenseless travelling Tibetans.
I, too, had to stay several days against my will.

One night, while dreaming in a light sleep,
Two beautiful brahmin girls of authentic being,
Wearing the brahminical thread,
Smiling coyly, and glancing out of the corners of their eyes,
Came before me and said,
"You must go to Sri Parvata in the South!"
I said, "I have never gone there before;
I don't even know the way."
The two girls replied,
"Brother, you don't have to do anything difficult;
We shall carry you on our shoulders."
They put me on the seat of a cloth palanquin
And lifted it into the sky like a parasol.
Like a flash of lightning, in a mere instant of time,
I dreamt that I arrived at Sri Parvata in the South.

In the cool shade of a grove of plaksa trees,
On a tira corpse seat
Sat Lord Saraha, the Great Brahmin.
I had never before seen such majestic brilliance.
He was flanked by two queens.
His body was adorned with charnel ground ornaments.
His joyous face was beaming.

"Welcome, my son!" he said.
Seeing the lord, I was overwhelmed with joy.
The hairs of my body stood on end, and I was moved to tears.
I circumambulated him seven times and I offered a full
prostration.

I received the soles of his feet on the top of my head.
"Father, accept me with kindness," I supplicated.

He blessed my body with his.
The moment he touched his hand to the top of my head,
My body was intoxicated with undefiled bliss.
Like an elephant drunk with liquor,
There dawned an experience of immovability.

He blessed my speech with his.
With the lion's roar of emptiness,
He spoke "that without letter."
Like a dream dreamt by a mute,
There dawned an experience beyond words.

He blessed my mind with his.
I realised the co-emergent dharmakaya,
That which neither comes nor goes.
Like a human corpse left in a charnel ground,
There dawned an experience of non-thought.

Then the pure speech of great bliss arose
From the vase of his precious throat.
With sign speech in the melody of Brahma,
He sang this vajra song which points out things as they are,
The meaning of an empty sky free from clouds.
Thus I heard this unborn self-utterance:

"NAMO Compassion and emptiness are inseparable.

This uninterrupted flowing innate mind
Is suchness, primordially pure.
Space is seen in intercourse with space.
Because the root resides at home,
Mind consciousness is imprisoned.
Meditating on this, subsequent thoughts
Are not patched together in the mind.
Knowing the phenomenal world is the nature of mind,
Meditation requires no further antidote.
The nature of mind cannot be thought.
Rest in this natural state.
When you see this truth, you will be liberated.
Just as a child would, watch the behaviour of barbarians.
Be carefree; eat flesh; be a madman.

"Just like a fearless lion,
Let your elephant mind wander free.
See the bees hovering among the flowers.
Not viewing samsara as wrong,
There is no such thing as attaining nirvana.
This is the way of ordinary mind.
Rest in natural freshness.
Do not think of activities.
Do not cling to one side or one direction.
Look into the midst of the space of simplicity."

Going beyond the exhausting of dharmata is the essential truth,
The summit of views, mahamudra.
This sign meaning, which pierces to the pith of mind,

I heard from the mouth of the Great Brahmin.

At that instant, I awoke.
I was caught by the iron hook of this unforgettable memory.
Within the dungeon of ignorant sleep,
The vision of insight-wisdom opened up
And the sun dawned in a cloudless sky,
Clearing the darkness of confusion.
I thought, "Even if I met the buddhas of the three times,
From now on, I would have nothing to ask them."

This was a decisive experience.
Discursive thoughts were exhausted, what a wonder!
E ma! The prophecies of yidams and dakinis
And the profound truth spoken by the guru,
Although I have been told not to speak of these things,
Tonight I cannot help but speak them.
Except for this very occasion,
I have never said this before.
Listen with your ears and repeat it at a later time.

I am a man who has travelled a long way
Without intimate friends and relatives.
Now, when my body becomes tired and hungry,
Son, what you have done will be in my mind.
I will not forget this; it is impressed deeply in my mind.
My heart friend, your kindness is repaid.

The lords who dwell above, the gurus,

The divine yidams who bestow siddhis,
And the dharmapalas who clear obstacles,
May all these please not scold me.
Please forgive me if there is any confusion in what I have said.

By the time Marpa finished singing the song, the words had struck deeply in the heart of the Prince, and all those who heard him. As he opened his eyes once again the Prince of Lokya felt that he was not looking at Lord Marpa, but at the Buddha in person before him.

Marpa in Tibet

Marpa soon started off on his journey once again and he travelled to Lhodrak. On the way, Marpa went to Nyo's house in Kharak to ask him for the books, which he had promised that he would lend earlier. As he reminded Nyo about his promise, Nyo offered him a measure of gold and a mandala. He then said, "Marpa, you are perhaps the most knowledgeable person about the Mahamaya. Why do you need the texts at all?" He kept talking in the same tone for a long while as Marpa patiently waited for him to finish. But at the end of it, Nyo did not lend the books that he said he would.

Marpa now wanted to visit India very desperately. He first went to Lhodrak, where he learnt that his father and mother had passed away. His old teacher and his elder brother welcomed him warmly. Since Marpa had been his student a while back, therefore his teacher did not ask Marpa to offer him a discourse, but he did make it clear that he held Marpa in great respect. As a matter of fact, no one in the village asked him for a discourse, but they all held him in high esteem and they all expressed their feeling of respect for him.

However, t'iere were many people who came to meet him from far away to Lhodrak and they wanted him to explain his teachings to them. They also brought with them several gifts and offered prostrations to him. To these people, Marpa gave various instructions and taught various sadhanas, as also the ritual traditions. Marpa then took some of these students as his attendants, to travel with him in search of gold. This time Marpa also took several abhisheka implements and other shrine objects with him when he started his journey.

Marpa commandeered a horse and travelled first to central Tibet, South of the Tsangpo River. As he stopped by the river and started to eat his meal, two tantric priests came to him. From their appearances, Marpa could make out that they were teachers. The one who looked to be the chief priest approached Marpa and asked, "Holy people, where are you coming from and where will you go from here?"

One of Marpa's students replied, "My lords, this person, our guru, is someone that you may have heard about. He is the close disciple of Mahapandit Naropa of India and he himself is Marpa Lotsawa, the great translator. Lord Marpa has asked us to travel with him as he frees those worthy souls who have fortunate karma and also wishes to establish karmic connections with people who are less fortunate. The real reason for our travel is that Lord Marpa wishes to return to India to engross himself in further studies and therefore we too are travelling with him collecting offerings of gold and other provisions."

As the student finished what he had to say, the chief smiled and said, "Oh, I have indeed heard a lot about your guru and have always had the fondest wish that I should be able to meet him one day. I would be honoured if you all could come and spend the night in my house and bless us all with your gracious presence."

In this way, Marpa was able to reach the monastery of Soaring Garuda Mountain in the region of Shung. The priest later turned out to be Marpa's chief disciple. His name was Ngokton Chodor of Shung and he served Marpa very well during his stay at the monastery. As a matter of fact, Marpa was so pleased with him that he even gave him the abhisheka and sadhana of Bhagavat Hevajra according to the teacher Padmavajra. Ngokton also made several humble offerings of fine clothing and myriad other things that Marpa accepted humbly. Marpa was so delighted with the people of the monastery that he asked his own disciples to attend the discourses and teachings of the monastery. He himself stayed there for nearly two months, teaching the people there about Dharma. During this period, Marpa's fame spread far and wide.

Marpa the Great Master

M arpa then went on to Sesamar in the region of Phen. It was at Sesamar that Marpa had the fortune of healing nine women of the disease of 'infant death'. He used the means of Kila. The ladies in turn were so indebted to Marpa that they gave him eleven measures of gold for every cure. Marpa even displayed the permission-blessing of Devi Remati (Kali) and also showed the people several yogic applications which they could carry out in their daily lives. During his whole stay there, he also taught the people several Dharma courses and they all accepted Marpa as their great master.

During that time in Tibet, no translators were allowed to give word-for-word literal translations of teachings. They had to first practice, and reach some realisation of the inner meaning of the teachings. Literal translations only gave one the shallow, surface meanings of what was taught, whereas 'tasting the flavour of the realisation,' as is the saying, gave the translator the real experience of the hard work and fulfillment of the actual practice. Only then were the translators allowed to actually translate, as they brought experience and understanding to the words. Marpa was one such dedicated translator, who was revered as the great master translator.

During his stay at Sesamara, one day, Marpa gave the abhisheka of Hevajra to the people of the place. At about the same time, a merchant Marpa Golek arrived in central Tibet from Nyingtrung, in the Damsho district of the North. He was surprised to see the huge crowd that had gathered by the hillside and he desired to know the reason. He was then informed about Marpa and told that at that very moment, Marpa, the great disciple of Naropa, was giving abhisheka and was now in the process of performing a ganacakra.

Seeing that their names were similar, Marpa Golek immediately assumed that they could be related. He thought to himself, "He is a great guru it seems. I should ask him to teach me about the various facts of life as well."

While he saw Marpa conduct the festivities, a deep faith for the religious man arose in Marpa Golek's heart. When he was finally able to seek a private audience with Marpa, he learnt about Marpa's quest for gold. He informed Marpa that he would never be able to find the gold that he needed from the Phen region of the country. He also informed him of how the people of Phen were also very dishonest and assured him that he would meet quite the other treatment from the people who lived in the eight districts up in the North.

Marpa assured Marpa Golek that if he were ever to receive an invitation from the people in the North that he spoke of, then he would surely pay them a visit.

As soon as Marpa Golek was able to complete his business, he returned to the North with haste. Once he was back home, he lost little time in arranging a welcoming party to go and invite Marpa to his village. He sent a fine horse with fine clothing and provisions, for the noble guru for his journey.

Very soon he received the news that Marpa was indeed very close to the village and that the party would reach the village soon. Hearing this bit of news, Marpa Golek immediately mounted his own horse and rode ahead to meet the guru and to accompany him to the village. He rode on to the border near Tsul in Dam and saw the party approaching. But he was shocked to see that Marpa still had his old clothes on and that he had not touched the new clothes that had been sent to him. Once he was able to reach Marpa, after welcoming him warmly, he said, "Sir, we in the North are very particular about appearances. May I request you to put away your old clothes and wear the new clothes that I had sent you with the welcoming party?"

Marpa heard him out and informed him that his own guru Naropa had actually blessed the clothes that he wore, and therefore he would not have the heart to throw them away. Rather, he mentioned to Marpa Golek, that keeping with the customs in the North, he would store his old clothes and wear the new ones that Golek had sent him and also the clothes that had been given to him by the people in the monastery.

Marpa Golek rode ahead to meet the guru.

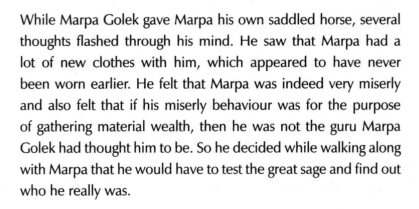

While Marpa Golek gave Marpa his own saddled horse, several thoughts flashed through his mind. He saw that Marpa had a lot of new clothes with him, which appeared to have never been worn earlier. He felt that Marpa was indeed very miserly and also felt that if his miserly behaviour was for the purpose of gathering material wealth, then he was not the guru Marpa Golek had thought him to be. So he decided while walking along with Marpa that he would have to test the great sage and find out who he really was.

He turned to Marpa and put the same question about the clothes to him. "Why do you not wear these clothes that people offer you?" he asked. Marpa could only smile at this question and said, "As I have informed you earlier, I am looking for gold which I will take to India to learn new teachings. If I do not have the gold then my whole voyage to India will be of waste. And it is but common knowledge that old clothes cannot be exchanged for gold, but new clothes can be. So I keep all the clothes that are offered to me, hoping that one day I will be able to exchange them for gold."

This answer lit up Marpa Golek from within. He was ashamed to have doubted this great man. He knew that this desire for material wealth was not a sin, but a great virtue. From that moment onwards, Marpa Golek became one of Marpa's greatest disciples, who took a vow standing there that he would always attend to his master during his entire visit.

Marpa's stay at Nyingtrung was most pleasurable. Marpa Golek fulfilled his vow by entering the gates of Dharma and requesting

Marpa for abhisheka and oral instructions. Marpa cured many cases of infant deaths in the province and he earned a lot of gold for his journey to India. Then Marpa also went to the gold rock of Mera in the North and was able to get a lot of gold for himself. As for Marpa Golek, not only did he give Marpa eighteen measures of gold, he also gave Marpa horses, cattle, sheep, suits of armor and even his own horse. Now Marpa realised that he had enough gold and other provisions with him and that it was now time for him to make his journey to India.

Marpa left along with Golek and some more of his disciples and they went to Lhodrak. Once they had crossed the Tsangpo River, they were met by Tsurton Wangnge of Tol, who welcomed them warmly. He even invited them to come with him to Tol. Marpa was so impressed with Tsurton's devotion that he blessed him with the abhisheka. Tsurton requested for the oral instructions of Guhyasamaja, but since Marpa was in a hurry to reach India, this could not be done. Tsurton then decided to accompany Marpa on his travels thereafter.

Marpa once again reached Shung were Ngopka welcomed them warmly. He made several offerings of gold and clothing to Marpa and also decided that he would accompany Marpa as his attendant. From there on, they journeyed to Trowo valley, where Bawachen of Parang invited them to South Layak. Marpa was very happy at the devotion of Bawachen and offered him the abhisheka of Mahamaya and he in turn gave Marpa several other gifts, which the great guru accepted humbly.

Finally it was time for Marpa to bid them all farewell. He

organised a huge ganacakra for his disciples. There they asked him about the gurus that he had in India. They also wanted to know about the guru who possessed the wondrous siddhi. They wanted to know everything about his journey to India, about the oral instructions and abhishekas that he received there and also about the companions that he had with him.

Marpa explained to them that since they had asked him several questions, the best way to answer them would be through a song. So saying, Marpa sang:

Lord Vajradhara of this age of strife,
Supreme being who has accomplished ascetic discipline,
Carried by everyone like a crown on his head,
Glorious Naropa, I respectfully pay homage at your feet.
This Marpa Lotsawa of Lhodrak
Met with Dharma when twelve years old.
This certainly reawakened the predispositions from former training.
First I learned the letters of the alphabet.
Then I learned the translation of words.
Finally I went South to Nepal and India.

I stayed three years in central Nepal.
From blessed Nepalese gurus
I heard the Catuhpitha, renowned as a powerful tantra.
I received the devi Vetali as a protector.

Not satisfied by this alone,

I went to India for further teachings.
I crossed poisonous and deadly rivers.
My skin shed like a snake's.

Daring to abandon my life for the sake of Dharma,
I arrived at that wonderful place prophesied by the dakinis,
Pullahari in the North.
At this monastery imbued with siddhi,
From the gatekeeper Mahapandit Naropa
I received the tantra of Hevajra, renowned for its profundity,
And the oral instructions of the union of mixing and ejecting.
I especially requested the karmamudra of candall
And received transmission of the hearing lineage.

At the monastery of Laksetra in the West
I touched the feet of glorious Jnanagarbha.
I listened to the father tantra, the Guhyasamaja,
Received the instructions of the illusory body and luminosity,
And learned the meaning of the path of five stages.
I went to the island in the boiling poison lake in the South.
In the middle of the day, it grew as dark as midnight.
Sometimes the path was clear and sometimes it disappeared.
Abandoning my fear of death, I searched for the jetsun.
I met glorious Santibhadra in person.
He gave me the mother tantra, the Mahamaya.
I learned the meaning of the three yogas, form and so on,
And received the instructions of the tantra of three illusions.

In the East I crossed the Ganges, the river of siddhis.

At the monastery of the quaking mountain
I touched the feet of the lord, Master Maimpa,
And received the profound tantra, the
Manjusri-nama-sangiti.
Living in the realisation of the Dharma of mahamudra,
The nature and workings of actual mind were resolved.
I saw the essence of the meaning of ground dharmata.

Renowned throughout all Jambudvipa,
These are the lineage gurus of the four directions.

Also from wandering yogins in charnel grounds
And kusulus dwelling under trees,
Some of whom are completely unknown,
I received many short instructions in sampannakrama,
Wondrous sadhanas,
And countless oral instructions of yogic applications.

On the way back to Tibet, Nyo of Kharak accompanied me.
When we arrived in central Nepal
I, Marpa Lotsawa of Lhodrak,
And Nyo Lotsawa of Kharak
Discussed which lotsawa was more learned and had greater oral
instructions.

When crossing the border from Nepal to Tibet,
Nyo was richer in wealth and material goods.
When I arrived in the four parts of Lato,
I had attained equal renown as a translator.

When I came to the center of U and Tsang in Tibet,
I was famed for oral instructions.
Since I have met siddha gurus,
There is no question as to the greatness of these oral
instructions.
Since I do not hope for enlightenment from sophistry,
Those expounders of texts may do as they please.

Marpa's elder brother too was greatly impressed at Marpa's knowledge and he too devoted himself to Marpa. He offered him any property that the great man may have desired. Marpa now had great dignity, wealth, respect and his fame had started to reach far and wide. He married Dagmema. Very soon he was overjoyed to see the birth of his son Dharma Dode.

Marpa's Second Journey to India

Now that Marpa was ready to leave for India, he organised a huge feast for all the gurus, yidams, dharmapalas and protectors for all that they had done for him in the past. Then Marpa took around fifty bags of gold and started off for India. There were many of his attendants who also wished to travel with him further, but Marpa would not listen to it. He forbade them from travelling with him because he wanted to make the journey on his own.

He first arrived in Nepal after crossing the border. There he met Chitherpa and Paindapa once again. He took out some of the gold that he was carrying and presented it to them. They were very pleased with Marpa's devotion and they blessed him and even arranged for some attendants to accompany him to India. With these attendants Marpa reached India comfortably.

Marpa was soon reunited with Naropa. Both the great gurus were overjoyed to be in each other's company. When they finally finished greeting each other and discussing about their well-being, Marpa requested Naropa to once again instill him with the abhisheka of Hevajra in all three versions, also the Hevajramulatantra. And he then expressed his desire to go through the explanations of the Dakini-vajrapanjara-tantra, amongst several other such holy teachings. He desired that he be taught all of these scriptures with their commentary and oral instructions as well.

As Marpa finished, Naropa advised him to go to the other gurus that he had been to earlier as well. He explained that Marpa should visit them first and review with them all that he had learnt earlier. He also said that if Marpa had any doubts, he should see to it that they are solved completely. "After that you should request them to teach you new teachings," advised Naropa. He then went on to ask Marpa whom he would like to go to first and Marpa replied that he would first like to visit Maitripa.

So saying, Marpa went off to meet Maitripa. The great guru was very happy to see Marpa once again, and he was also pleased with the offering of gold that Marpa gave him. He reviewed all the teachings that he had given to Marpa earlier. Marpa then requested him to give him the abhisheka of the Guhyasamaja and the tantra of the Mahamudratilaka, and Maitripa was only too happy to oblige. Marpa copied all the texts once again as he had lost his previous copies because of Nyo's jealousy.

Marpa then went back to meet Naropa in Pullahari and after spending some time with him, he went on towards Nalanda. There he met the great Kashmiri pandit Sri Bhadra. While they assembled at the ganacakra, Sri Bhadra asked him about the instructions that he had received from Lord Maitripa. He then wanted to know whether the intention of the lineage of Lord Savari, disciple of the great Lord Brahmin, or the intention of his own guru Naropa, diciple of Tilopa, was more profound.

Marpa pondered over the question for a while and then said, "I think it would be better for me to answer your question through a song." And then Marpa sang:

Listen, heart friend Sri Bhadra!
I am a Buddhist called Marpa.
As you asked which is more profound,
The intention of Naropa or Maitripa,
This song is my reply.
Lion-like Naropa
Is the most precious of all.
His great intention
Is to fulfill all needs and desires.
Lord Dharmadhara, please accept us with kindness.

The lotus feet of this mahapandit
These days are my crest ornament.
His intention is as follows.
Please pay attention and listen carefully.

The sky of dharmakaya is thick with rain clouds of wisdom.
The continuous rain of emanations spreads over all beings.
To the supremely born guru of the uninterrupted lineage
I respectfully prostrate with body, speech, and mind.

The dharmakaya like the sky
Is the buddha, great Vajradhara.
The thick rain clouds of wisdom
Are the two bodhisattvas.

The amna rainfall of buddha activity
Is the jetsun, Brahmin Saraha.
The emanation who works for the benefit of beings
Is the Lord of Hermits, Savari.

The holder of this unbroken lineage
Is the Master, Prince Maitripa.
I received kindness from this holy one.
This is how to understand his intention.

Self-luminous unchanging insight
Is described as unborn dharmakaya.
Unceasing self-born wisdom
Is described as the multiplicity of nirmanakaya.

These two unified in co-emergence
Are described as the sambhogakaya.
These three free from origin
Are described as the svabhavikakaya.

All these, beyond conditions
Are described as the mahasukhakaya.
These are the five ultimate kayas.
Does this gladden your minds, heart friends?

This was how Marpa explained the functioning of the five kayas and Sri Bhadra was pleased with Marpa's answer.

Now Sri Bhadra also wanted to know about Marpa's views on meditation, action and fruition. Hearing this, Marpa once again sang out:

Please listen without your minds wandering.
Though I am not skilled in composing songs,
This is the way to understand the true oral instructions.
Keep this in mind and ponder it.
The three worlds are primordially pure.
Ultimately, there is nothing more to understand.
Not negation, unceasing continuity,
Unchanging—such is the view.

The innate essence is naturally luminous.
Unconditioned, meditation is unceasing.
Not negation, beyond losing and gaining,
Without desire or attachment—such is the meditation.

Arising from the natural occurrence of various coincidences,
The play of illusion is unobstructed.
Not negation,
Things are unpredictable, abrupt—such is the action.

Mind shines as bodhicitta.
There is no attainment of the three kayas of buddha.

Not negation, beyond hope and fear,
Without ground or root—such is the fruition.

This delighted Sri Bhadra even more and now he wanted to
know about Maitripa's method of teaching. He wanted to know
whether Maitripa would teach his oral instructions all at once,
or did he instruct them gradually through different techniques.
Marpa decided that the answer to this question lay in a song:

O you superior dharma friends!
My Jetsun Maitripa
Touched the feet of Savari,
The heart son of Nagarjuna, protector of beings,
Who was foretold by Avalokitesvara.
Savari gave him the full teachings of the three yanas.
He received the secret name Advayavajra.
He holds the keys of all the orders of tantra.
He accomplished the techniques of the secret mantra.

Victory banner of Dharma, treasury of Dharma,
Lion of Dharma, king of Dharma—
He is widely learned in philology, madhyamaka, and logic.
He attained the mastery of a pandit.
He knows faultlessly the reality of things as they are.

He abandoned his royal domain as if it were weeds
And attained the supreme state in one life.
Jetsun Dakini revealed herself to him
And so he received all the ordinary siddhis.

In this way he attained immeasurable virtues.
Now these are the intentions of the father:
To ordinary people who are receptive to the gradual path
He gives the oral instruction of candali for life force,
The oral instruction of illusory body for non-attachment,
The transmission of luminosity for clearing away darkness
The transmission of existence as sambhogakaya,
The transmission of birth as nirmanakaya, and so on.
Thus he guides them through the supreme means of ground, path,
and fruition.

To those who are receptive to the sudden path,
He transmits naked mahamudra.
Seeing this father fills one's body, speech, and mind with faith.
Hearing him purifies karmic obscurations.
Meeting him liberates one from the terrors of the lower realms.
If requested, he places buddha in the palm of one's hand.
Holding the lineage of the glorious Lord of Hermits.
Mahapandit Naropa's heart son,
The precious second Buddha,
Lord Maitripa possesses these virtues.

These days people are extremely jealous.
If this is repeated to anyone other than you, friends
Virtue will not flourish and defilement will increase
Therefore, keep this secret from ordinary people.
These are the actions of the guru.
Isn't this good, fortunate vajra friends?

And so saying, Marpa concluded his answer.

Marpa stayed on at Nalanda for some more time and then decided to go back to meet Naropa once again to let him know about the progress that he had made in the review of his earlier teachings.

After spending some time with Naropa, Marpa once again made his way to meet some more gurus, along with the gold that he had brought as an offering. On the island in poison lake he met Kukuripa, as well as the yogini with bone ornaments. From there he travelled all the way to Laksetra in the West and met Jnana-garbha and Simhadvipa. He made his offerings in gold and in return, they once again instructed all the abhishekas to him. Marpa noted down all that he learnt from his gurus and returned to Pullahari once again.

Now Naropa too offered him several scrolls and oral instructions on the Cakrasamvara of the lineage of King Indrabhiiti and also explained the Buddhakapila-tantra to Marpa, in the tradition of Saraha. Marpa translated all this and made copious notes of these immortal instructions.

One day, as Naropa and Marpa were busy partaking their meals, a pandit from Labar in Kashmir, called Akarasiddhi came to meet them. Marpa noted how Naropa greeted him as an equal. But Akarasiddhi on the other hand prostrated before Naropa and requested the great guru to instruct him on the abhisheka, commentary and oral instructions of the Guhyasamaja. Naropa was only too happy to oblige and made a full discourse on the subject. Even Marpa paid attention and learnt these instructions as well.

Once the instructions were over, Akarasiddhi decided to take his leave. As Marpa bid him farewell, he asked him where the great guru would be headed for now. Akarasiddhi informed him that he was on his way through Tibet to a pilgrimage to Wu-tai Shan in China. Marpa thought that once Akarasiddhi reached Tibet, he would teach the Guhyasamaja himself and no one would come to Marpa for these instructions. Akarasiddhi understood what was going through Marpa's mind, but he said nothing. Soon he set off for his long journey.

As Akarasiddhi arrived in Knap Kungthang, he met Naktso Lotsawa there. When Naktso greeted him and welcomed him to the town, he learnt that the guru was headed for Wu-tai Shan in China. But Naktso merely laughed at his appearance and declared how he always despised Indian pandits who wander through the lands bare-feet, looking for gold. He then went on to ask if he knew the great pandit Akarasiddhi. The answer changed Naktso's stance completely. He mentioned, "You then surely are not looking for gold. I welcome you even more warmly now because I know that your heart is true."

As they got together and started discussing about the great teachings, Naktso requested Akarasiddhi to instruct him about the Guhyasamaja. Akarasiddhi was only too happy to explain the whole text to Naktso, but then he realised that he was not karmically connected to the people of Tibet. He realised that only Marpa Lotsawa could tame the people there and therefore he decided, that instead of going to China, he would return to India.

Naktso however was very pleased with Akarasiddhi's knowledge and he made several offerings of gold to the learned guru. He also offered many attendants for the great sage, who would accompany him on his journey to Lhasa. But Akarasiddhi informed him that he had decided to go back to India and therefore, he did not need any gold or companions.

Naktso requested Akarasiddhi to tell him the reason for changing his mind and Akarasiddhi explained that he had received the answer through his higher perception. But Naktso was insistent that Akarasiddhi accept the gold so that he could perfect the accumulations. It was only for this reason that Akarasiddhi accepted a small amount of the offerings.

Now that Naktso Lotsawa was also experienced in the sacred outlook, he too realised that Marpa was indeed one of the great Boddhisattvas dwelling on the earth at the moment.

When Akarasiddhi returned to India he met Marpa and told him that he had left the taming of the whole of Tibet to Marpa. At first Marpa was worried that Akarasiddhi had learnt of the thoughts that Marpa had in his mind regarding his visit to Tibet through his higher perceptions, but later on realised that he had nothing to be ashamed of, as there was no breach of trust on his part.

But Marpa did agree that he should try and keep his mind clear of such negative thoughts in future, and he confessed about the same to the great pandit.

Marpa resumed studying the abhishekas and oral instructions that he had come to learn in India and was able to finish his studies in a short while.

Now it was once again time for Marpa to return to Tibet. He organised a great ganacakra in honour of Naropa. Naropa was so pleased with Marpa's devotion that he placed his hand on Marpa's head and sang:

A flower blooming in the sky,
The son of a barren woman rides a horse
Wielding a whip of tortoise hair.
With the dagger of a hare's horn
He kills his enemy in the space of dharmata.
The mute speaks, the blind man sees.
The deaf man hears, the cripple runs.
The sun and moon dance, blowing trumpets.
The little child turns the wheel.

Naropa then informed Marpa that there were some more teachings that the great guru was yet to convey to his disciple and therefore urged Marpa to return once again. Marpa did not ask his teacher the meaning of the song and vowed that he would surely return to India soon. With these words, Marpa started off on his journey to Tibet once again.

Marpa Returns to Tibet

Once again, Marpa crossed through Nepal and was soon in Tibet. He arrived at Tsang and the great Metbn Tsonpo of Tsangrong asked Marpa to instruct to him the abhisheka of the Cakrasamvara. So Marpa stayed on at Tsangrong.

Soon Marpa's disciples in Trowo came to know of their guru's return and that he was in good health. Led by Marpa Golek they immediately started off to meet him. As they were travelling, they met Marpa on the mountains of upper Nyang, on his way from Tsangrong. So, they returned and went to Lhodrak.

Marpa's fame spread far and wide and soon he had many disciples. It was at this time that the building of the tower of Sekhar and the taming of Jetsun Milarepa happened.

Marpa's son, Dharma Dode had grown up. A consecration ceremony was held, where Marpa and Dharma Dode engaged each other in a debate. Dharma Dode was declared the winner, when he revealed that it was indeed his father who had done all the hard work, but it was him who had the practices; just like stirring of the ladle is hard work, but the ladle gets to carry the soup!

But Marpa was quick to respond, saying that the son was learned and great because of the father's kindness. He asked his son to not be proud and sung him a song of urgent command immediately:

Listen noble son, Dodebum.
Though you say you are learned and great,
All that is the noble father's kindness.
Gathering vast accumulations through former lives,
I created wealth of yellow gold.
Thus I pleased the guru.
Listen noble son, Dodebum.
Naropa, Maitripa, and Path of Liberation
Are the three holy root gurus.
Thus the oral instructions are profound.

Listen noble son, Dodebum.
Because I never irritated the gurus,
The dakinis were pleased and cared for me like a child.
Thus I was free from obstacles and bad circumstances.
I trained my mind in the holy Dharma of mahayana.
Arousing bodhicitta, I encompassed all beings.
Thus I spread the holy Dharma in Tibet.

Listen noble son, Dodebum.
Since I went forth to greet the guru on his arrival and escorted

him on his departure,
The soles of my feet were marked with dharmacakras.
Thus I travelled through India.

Listen noble son, Dodebum.
As for the tantras, commentaries, and oral instructions,
I learned their words and meanings thoroughly, without error.
Thus I spread the teachings.

Listen noble son, Dodebum.
Meton, Ngokton, Tsurion, and Goiek
Are the four heart sons.
Thus I taught the tantras and commentaries.

Listen noble son, Dodebum.
He who accomplished whatever the guru said
Is Mila Dorje Gyaltsen.
Thus I bestowed the oral instructions on him.

Listen noble son, Dodebum.
I, the lord father, am getting old.
I have arrived at the exhausting of dharmata.
Dode, your time has come.
By your great learning, propagate the teachings.
Fulfil the wish of this old man.

Once the consecration and invocations of auspiciousness were concluded, Marpa sang another song on the benediction of auspiciousness:

I supplicate the kind gurus.
This precious lineage of mine
Is auspicious, free from degradation.
May the goodness of this auspiciousness be present.
The direct path of the profound oral instructions
Is auspicious, free from corruption or confusion.
May the goodness of this auspiciousness be present.

I, Marpa Lotsawa,
Have the auspicious profound pith.
May the goodness of this auspiciousness be present.

Gurus, yidams, and dakinis
Have auspicious blessings and siddhis.
May the goodness of this auspiciousness be present.

Great sons and assemblies of disciples
Have auspicious faith and samaya.
May the goodness of this auspiciousness be present.

Benefactors from countries near and far
Have the auspicious harmonious occasion to gather merit.
May the goodness of this auspiciousness be present.

All deeds and activities
Are auspicious, enlightened, and benefit beings.
May the goodness of this auspiciousness be present.

Gods and demons of the phenomenal world

Are auspiciously under powerful command.
May the goodness of this auspiciousness be present.

The crowds of gods and men gathered here
Auspiciously aspire to bliss and happiness.
May the goodness of this auspiciousness be present.

His song moved all those who gathered there and they all made several offerings to Marpa. Marpa accepted the gifts humbly and hoped that the virtue of enlightenment would befall on all of them.

Jetsun Milarepa had now become a student of Marpa and Marpa gave him the necessary abhishekas and oral instructions. He then asked his student to retreat at Taknya in Lhodrak. All this while, Marpa's mind was constantly reminded of the promise that he had made to Naropa about returning to India once again and meeting his great guru.

In order to prepare for the journey to India, Marpa left for Northern Uru along with Marpa Golek and some more of his disciples in search of gold.

Marpa's fame had spread far and wide by now and many people came to him for guidance and teachings. Marpa received a lot of gifts from them. Marpa even performed an abhisheka at the house of Marpa Golek. While he was just about to conclude the abhisheka, a strange feeling swept over Marpa and he went into a trance like state. There he saw a vision.

He saw three beautiful maidens dressed in silks, standing before him. They were singing the coded verses of Mahapandit Naropa, which Marpa had not been able to understand till now. Suddenly the meaning of Naropa's teachings became very clear in the song:

The dakini is the flower blooming in the sky.
The son of a barren woman riding a horse is the hearing lineage.
The whip of tortoise hair is the inexpressible.
The dagger of a hare's horn is the unborn.
This kills Tilopa in the space of dharmata.
Tilopa is the mute, beyond word, thought, and expression.
Naropa is the blind man, liberated in seeing the truth of nothing to see.
Naropa is the deaf man, the dharmakaya mountain of dharmata.
Lodro is the cripple, who runs on the mountain with the gait of luminosity, free from coming and going.
The moon and sun are Hevajra and consort.
They are two dancers, but one taste.
The trumpets proclaiming fame in the ten directions sound for worthy vessels.
The wheel is Cakrasamvara. Its turning is the hearing lineage wheel itself.
O child, turn it without attachment.

Just at that moment Marpa woke up with tears in his eyes. His disciples were all around him. Marpa said, "I have to leave tomorrow. I cannot wait any longer. I have to see the glorious Naropa immediately."

So Marpa started making arrangements for his departure. Later on, his disciples, led by Marpa Golek asked him the reason for his hasty departure. Marpa explained all that had seen in his trance. Marpa Golek understood the whole matter and declared that seeing the urgency of the situation he would supply Marpa with all the gold that he needed to make the journey possible. Soon Marpa started off for Lhodrak along with Marpa Golek and some more of his disciples, and he stayed there for some time.

At about the same time, Milarepa too had a vision one night about a beautiful lady who was clothed in silk and was sky blue in colour. She told him that he had the Mahamudra and the six yogas of Naropa, which would help him attain the state of Buddhahood through a prolonged process. However, she declared that he did not know about the teachings of ejection and transference of consciousness, which would help him attain the state much sooner, with lesser effort.

Milarepa soon went to Lhodrak and told Marpa about the vision that he had. Marpa in turn told him about what Naropa had told him when he had left India the last time. He had told him about the transference of consciousness, an instruction he was to learn the next time he came to India. Both master and disciple went through all the texts that Marpa had; and found mention on ejection of consciousness, but nowhere could they find any text on transference of consciousness.

Marpa realised that he now needed to visit India very soon. He received strict opposition from his wife and some disciples, who cited his old age as an obstacle to make the tedious journey. But

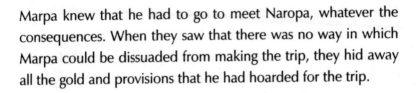

Marpa knew that he had to go to meet Naropa, whatever the consequences. When they saw that there was no way in which Marpa could be dissuaded from making the trip, they hid away all the gold and provisions that he had hoarded for the trip.

However, the next morning, Marpa could not be found anywhere. Finally Milarepa was able to find Marpa and all his disciples came running there to beg for his forgiveness. Marpa was adamant. "With the gold, or without the gold, I will have to go and meet my guru."

Even though it was time for Marpa to leave for India, his students decided to entreat him once again from going. They mentioned that there were areas in the journey where even horses broke down in fatigue and his old age would definitely act as a hindrance. They explained that if something were to happen to him they would be lost.

But Marpa explained that all they had to do was practise the Dharma that they had been taught in Tibet. But his students kept insisting that he should instead send his son, Dharma Dode, and his attendants to meet Naropa and bring back the instructions for him. They all wished that their guru would not leave them and go.

But Marpa again said that he would have to go because he had given Naropa his word that he would come and meet him one more time and therefore he would have to keep his word. He also mentioned that he could not send his son because he had told Naropa that he would come himself and not send his son.

There were some teachings that he was still to learn from Naropa and therefore the journey had to be made. While he agreed that he was indeed older than he was earlier, he was not all that old that he could not make the journey to India. He was well aware of the way and the customs of the country and he knew what he had to do.

So saying, Marpa sang out a song on his going to India:

I pay homage at the feet of glorious Naropa and Maitripa.
The vow I have taken in the presence of Naropa
Makes it supremely necessary that I go.

Since I have been encouraged to go by solving the dakinis' code,
I have been overwhelmed by the memory of my guru.
Whatever the consequences may be, I am going to India.
Even at the cost of my life, I am going to India.

Although the great plain Paimo Palthang is vast,
I have the oral instructions in how consciousness rides prana.
No ordinary steed is a match for this.
Whatever the consequences may be, I am going to India.
Even at the cost of my life, I am going to India.

Although the snow pass Khala Chela is very cold,
I have the oral instructions of the blazing fire of candali.
Ordinary woollen clothing is no match for this.
Whatever the consequences may be, I am going to India.
Even at the cost of my life, I am going to India.

Although Nepal is very hot,
I have the oral instructions in equalizing the elements.
The ordinary six precious substances are no match for this.
Whatever the consequences may be, I am going to India.
Even at the cost of my life, I am going to India.

Although the Ganges river is wide and deep,
I have the oral instructions of consciousness soaring in space.
No ordinary boat is a match for this.
Whatever the consequences may be, I am going to India.
Even at the cost of my life, I am going to India.

Although the primitive borderlands of India have great famine,
I have the oral instructions in how to live on the water of
asceticism.
Ordinary food and drink are no match for this.
Whatever the consequences may be, I am going to India.
Even at the cost of my life, I am going to India.

Although there are great dangers on the road and in the small
outlying districts,
I have the oral instructions in mamos who paralye bandits.
Ordinary escorts are no match for this.
Whatever the consequences may be, I am going to India.
Even at the cost of my life, I am going to India.

The gurus Naropa and Maitripa live in India.
Sri Santibhadra lives in India,
And the shrine of Mahabodhi is in India.

Whatever the consequences may be, I am going to India.
Even at the cost of my life, I am going to India.

Marpa then gathered all the gold and provisions that he had accumulated for his journey. He refused to take anyone with him on his journey and soon left for India.

Last Trip to India

As Marpa began his journey, he was overjoyed to meet Lord Atisha at Langpona at Sheng in upper Nyang. Lord Atisha had been the person in charge of discipline at Nalanda when Marpa had arrived there to learn the various abhishekas. He was a kind and gentle man and Marpa was very happy to have met him while he had started off on his auspicious journey to meet Naropa.

Lord Atisha was planning to go to Tibet, where he wanted to spread the teachings of the Buddha. He was at that moment offering the Vajramala abhisheka to some disciples there and Marpa too supplicated before the great Lord and learnt the abhisheka.

On being asked about Naropa and his whereabouts, Atisha told Marpa that Naropa had now entered the ganacakra of spiritual beings and he had stopped meeting human beings. He advised Marpa to accompany him as a translator to Tibet because there was hardly any possibility of his meeting Naropa in India.

But Marpa informed Atisha that even though he would not be

able to meet Naropa, he would still have to go to India once and make an attempt to meet his great guru. Since he had made the vow to Naropa, Marpa decided that he had to keep it.

Even as he met gurus Paindapa and Chitherpa in Nepal, he received the same news about Naropa, but Marpa was adamant that he had to complete his journey, though his chances of meeting Naropa seemed rather bleak.

Seeing his devotion, the two spiritual masters told him that since he kept samaya and had the eye of Dharma, there was the possibility of his meeting Naropa. They advised him to offer ganacakras and were confident that Naropa would surely come to meet him.

Finally, when Marpa reached India, he was greeted by Prajnasimha, who told him that in the previous year on the full moon of the New Year, Naropa had entered the action and was in the spiritual world now. Marpa saw that he had lost a lot of time collecting gold for the visit and wished that the dakinis had brought forth Naropa's message for him a little earlier. The finality of Naropa's absence now dawned on Marpa as he started to weep at this news.

He asked the great sramanera if Naropa had left any message for him, but all that could be learnt was that Naropa had confided in the sramanera that Marpa would definitely come. He had left with him his own vajra and ghanta and the image of yidam to give to Marpa. The vajra and the ghanta had been stolen, but Prajnasimha had been able to keep the image safe.

As Marpa received the painting of Hevajra, he started to cry remembering his guru. But the sramanera merely told him that because of the devotion that he had for Naropa, he was sure that the great jetsun would surely meet Marpa. So saying, he asked Marpa to arrange a feast with the gold that he had brought with him and then supplicate before the great guru. He also advised Marpa to visit Maitripa once.

Marpa acceded to the advice and immediately left to meet Maitripa. Reunited with his old guru, Marpa arranged for a grand feast and it was there that Maitripa's words assured him of meeting Naropa once again. Maitripa said:

I dreamt that the victory banner with a jewel finial fluttered,
A dancing girl looked at a mirror out of the corner of her eye,
A victory banner fluttered above a soaring bird,
And a captain sailed a ship.
You will definitely meet glorious Naropa.

Maitripa then told Marpa to go and visit Jetsun Sanribhadra who was first Naropa's master and then became his disciple. He told Marpa to stay with him for a month and receive instructions from him.

Marpa did as he was told and stayed a month with Sanribhadra. As the time came to an end, Sanribhadra told Marpa:

I dreamt that the jetsun, glorious Naropa,
Gazing like an elephant,
With his eyes the sun and moon,

Sent light rays to Tibet.
You will meet Naropa.

Then on Sanribhadra's advice, Marpa travelled to the Yogini adorned with bone ornaments, who too was a disciple of Naropa and asked him to stay with her for a month. At the end of the month, she told Marpa:

I dreamt that trumpets sounded from three mountain peaks
And guided you from the confluence of three valleys.
A lamp burning inside a vase
Filled Jambudvipa with light.
You will meet Naropa.

Marpa then went back to sramanera Prajnasimha and stayed with him for a month, learning many instructions from him as well. At the end, Prajnasimha told him:

I dreamt that on the great plain of misery
I led a blind man and handed him over to someone else,
Who opened his ignorant eyes.
He looked at himself in the mirror of his mind.
You will meet Naropa.

From there, on Prajnasimha's advice, Marpa travelled to Naropa's Vajra brothers, Riripa and Kasoripa and stayed with them for a while, learning new teachings. Then at the end of it, Riripa told him:

Just as formerly the Kulika Dharmaraja
Supplicated the Brahmin Bhadrika,

Witnessed by Kalyana and Bhadra,
Just so you will attain the fruition of meeting Naropa.

Kasoripa too had more or less the same words to tell Marpa, as he said:

At immovable Pullahari,
The pure mandala of the moon,
Naropa will show you
The dharmakaya mirror of mind.

Marpa realised that since all these great gurus sang to him about prophecies of meeting Naropa again, he knew that he would surely be able to meet his guru once again.

Marpa could not remain in one place for long, as he wanted to meet Naropa at the earliest. Therefore he started travelling all over the country in search of the jetsun. There was also an incident when an evil king in the East, who wanted the gold that Marpa was carrying, arrested him. But the minute he was brought before the king, Marpa declared that he was going in search of his guru and could not waste his time waiting there. The king had a change of heart at this statement and sent Marpa away with some more food and provisions. As per the king's suggestion, Marpa travelled to the East for eight months in search of Naropa.

In Search of Naropa

In the first month of his travels, Marpa saw Naropa in his dreams one night, riding on a lion and flanked by two escorts called Jnanamati and Gunasiddhi. He saw that they were all singing and dancing on the sun and the moon.

He then heard the two yoginis tell him:

Naropa is non-dual unity.
Flanked by two consorts,
He rides a lion
And sings and dances on the sun and moon.
Are you not deceived by the confusion of dream?

Marpa would mostly go out in search of Naropa on his own, or would take someone along with him at times. In the second month, guru Paindapa arrived in India and Marpa took him along on his search. But they could not find Naropa. When they were exhausted, a voice from the sky said:

If the horse of continual devotion

Is not urged on by the whip of exertion,
Like the deer of grasping and fixation
Are you not caught in the trap of reality, wandering in samsara?

But in the third month of his travels, some good fortune was bestowed on Marpa. He met a herdsman who declared that he had seen Naropa. Rewarding the man handsomely, Marpa set off in search. Soon he was able to see Naropa's footprints, and on touching that dust to his forehead, he heard a voice tell him:

The footprint is like the imprint of a bird in the sky.
If you do not recognize this free from reference point,
Like a dog chasing the shadow of a flying bird
Won't you stray into the abyss of futility?

Finally, in the fourth month of his travels, Marpa saw a yogi clad in a yellow robe walking down a mountain. Marpa strained to see who the man was, hoping that he would now be reunited with his guru, when suddenly he heard Naropa say:

If you do not loose the snake knot of doubt
In the dharmakaya, the dharmata of mind
In which all is unborn,
You will not accomplish your purpose with a double-pointed needle.

No sooner were the words uttered that Naropa disappeared.

The same thing happened once again in the fifth month, when

Marpa was able to catch a glimpse of Naropa's face and once again his guru said:

Like a rainbow, the body is free from attachment.
If you do not recognize this free from reference point,
Like a blind man sightseeing
How can you understand the truth?

And like last time, Naropa disappeared after saying these words.

In the sixth month again, Marpa had a vision of Naropa sitting in a sandy barren place. On seeing his great guru, Marpa immediately supplicated before him and made offerings of gold to him. He even wanted Naropa to instruct him in some more teachings, when Naropa said:

Since apparent existence is primordially pure,
If you do not offer the mandala of dharmata.
But rather this mandala of precious metal to which you are attached,
Are you not chained by the eight worldly dharmas?

And once again Naropa was lost.

In the seventh month, Marpa had a vision of Naropa sitting in a cave and removing the organs of a corpse. Removing the brains and the ribs, Naropa started eating them. Marpa once again supplicated before Naropa and requested for some more teachings. But Naropa merely handed Marpa some ribs – who was nauseated at the ghastly sight and was unable to eat. Naropa then said:

In the great vessel of great bliss,
Great bliss and enjoyment are pure in equal taste.
If you do not enjoy this as great bliss,
The enjoyment of great bliss will not arise.

And then Marpa lost Naropa once again.

This time Marpa did not want to lose Naropa like the previous months and searched around the cave for him. But Naropa was nowhere to be found. Marpa then decided to eat the ribs his great teacher had given and found that they tasted like ambrosia.

Again, in the eighth month, Marpa had a vision of Naropa and he chased after him. However hard he tried, he could not manage to catch up with the old jetsun. But whenever Marpa would stop to rest, the old teacher too would sit down. Marpa realised that it was still not time for them to meet and therefore requested some oral instructions from Naropa. All Naropa said was:

If the horse of non-action, dharmata, and luminosity
Does not gallop free from coming and going,
Like a deer pursuing a mirage
Are you not wandering on the plane of futility?

That day Marpa had a long conversation with Naropa.

After these grueling eight months of arduous travel and fleeting

Mandala of the Bhagavat Hevajra of nine devis.

visions, Marpa was now tired and depressed. One day, he met a herdsman, who showed him Naropa's footprint on a crystal boulder. Giving him some gold as a reward, Marpa walked off in that direction in search of his guru. As he walked along, he saw the mandala of the Bhagavat Hevajra of nine emanation devis on the top of a sandalwood tree. As he prostrated before the sight, he started to cry. The light streaming forth from the mandala dissolved into Marpa's heart, blessing his body and empowering his speech. Suddenly out of nowhere, appeared Naropa. He was adorned with charnel ground ornaments, and he possessed the nine moods of a heruka.

Naropa began by saying that the father had now arrived in front of the son. Seeing Naropa before him in person, Marpa started to weep with joy, as if he had attained the first bhumi.

Marpa now did not know what to do. He tried to place Naropa's feet on his head, then he tried to embrace his guru and finally, he fainted. When he awoke, he once again realised the situation he was in and made an offering of a mandala of gold.

But Naropa merely said, "It is not gold that I want." However much Marpa tried, Naropa would not even accept a single piece of the grand substance. When Marpa kept insisting, begging Naropa to take the gold, the Mahapandit finally accepted the offering in the name of the guru and the three jewels, and threw away all the gold into the forest. Though Marpa was overjoyed to be in Naropa's company once again, he did feel bad about Naropa throwing away the gold as he had had a real tough time collecting it in Tibet. Seeing his beloved student's face, Naropa closed and opened his fist, and the gold was back there. He then struck the ground with his foot and the land turned to gold. He said, "I do not need the gold. If I want, all this land is gold."

Naropa then declared that he would now have to organise a feast for his son. No sooner had he said the words, a fish came and fell before Marpa. On Naropa's orders, Marpa cut open the fish and out came the five meats, the five amritas and several other such ganacakra substances.

Once the feast was concluded, Marpa immediately requested Naropa to instruct him with more teachings. Naropa then informed Marpa that he was there because of Tilopa's kindness. Since Tilopa had given a command-prophecy, Naropa too would give the same, but in Pullahari.

Marpa wanted to know more about the command-prophecy, to which Naropa said:

With the sun of self-liberated wisdom,
At the monastery of Pullahari
Dispel the darkness of Man's ignorance.
Let the light of wisdom pervade everywhere.

Some dakinis were not very happy at this, as they were very possessive of the Dharma. They created obstructive spirits, who scared Marpa. As they reached Pullahari, Marpa begged Naropa to save him. Marpa kept very close to Naropa, walking through mountains in the process. Though Naropa had the powers to save Marpa, he merely called upon Tilopa, saying:

This son prophesied by the guru
Is the worthy vessel, Marpa Lodro.
Please bless him by removing the obstacles
Caused by these she-maras, so-called dakinis.

No sooner did Naropa utter these words that the manifestations of Tilopa came along, with immeasurable hosts of wrathful deities with their weapons. The demons that were scaring Marpa were sent off packing. Marpa also felt that he could see Tilopa's form in between the clouds and started dancing with joy. These footprints between the rocks can still be seen at Pullahari.

Once the demons were gone, Lord Marpa asked Naropa to instruct him with the hearing lineage and the ejection of transference of consciousness. Hearing that Marpa had met a student called Tubhaga in Tibet, who had received the revelation of these instructions from a dakini, Naropa's heart was filled with delight. "Beautiful! Even in the dark country of Tibet, there is a being like the sun rising over the snow."

So saying, Naropa sang:

In the pitch-black land of the North
Is one like the sun rising over the snow.
To this being known as Tubhaga
I prostrate.

After the song, Naropa started to teach Marpa these special teachings by the means of sand mandalas. Naropa performed the abhishekas of Cakrasamvara. From there on he participated in several such mandalas and abhishekas and Marpa soaked in his guru's revelations.

Naropa told Marpa: "If you attend to the oral instructions of these special teachings, the oral instructions given to you previously will be like the outer husk. These supreme oral instructions are the innermost essence. It should be a teaching restricted to a single lineage holder for thirteen generations. Give it to your student called Tubhaga and buddha activity will spread and flourish."

Naropa explained that had these instructions been given to Marpa right at the very beginning, he would have perhaps not needed to learn the instructions he had been given earlier. He then went on to add that anyhow the time was not appropriate in the previous two occasions of Marpa's visit, for giving these teachings. It was necessary to know about Marpa's inner being itself, before these lessons of the highest level could be conferred on him. The fact that he took the pains to collect the gold and make the gruelling journeys all the way from Tibet to India are alone witness to the fact that Marpa was a great soul. So saying, Naropa gave a ganacakra to Lord Marpa.

Naropa then supplicated to the three jewels so that they would protect Marpa from the obstacles of Mara. Marpa, on hearing this, asked Naropa if the three jewels would be kind enough to protect all sentient beings through the same way. Naropa was very happy at this thought and he extended his kindness as Marpa had requested.

Once Marpa was very ill and some vajra brothers and sisters

came to tend to him. But Marpa believed in the healing powers of Naropa and sent them away. He knew that if he had to die, there was nothing that could cure him. But he decided that till the moment death came, he would stay with Naropa, learning the instructions of higher consciousness and matters of spiritual enlightenment. When Marpa recovered, the vajra brothers and sisters organised a thanksgiving feast for him. Lord Naropa too was overjoyed and he sang a song, summarizing the six yogas:

I bow at the feet of the kind lord.
You, Marpa Lotsawa of Tibet,
With a free and well-favoured body
And a mind of sadness this summer, hear these words.

The method of resting the mind is confidence in the view.
The method of resting the body is the pith of meditation.
Outside is only the illusory form of devas.
Inside is just the three nadis and four cakras.
Below is the A stroke, candali.
Above is the form of the letter HAM.
Above and below are the wheels of prana.
Practice holding the life force in a vaselike manner.
In between the letters, experience bliss, emptiness, and luminosity.
This we call the oral instructions of candali.
Lotsawa, have you captured prana with precision?

Outer appearance is only illusion.
Inner experience is inexpressible.

Day and night, experiences are simply nirmanakaya.
This we call the oral instructions of illusory body.
Lotsawa, have you experienced revulsion towards attachment?

When experiencing the confusion of dreams,
Visualize at the throat the syllable OM radiating light.
Through the creation of habitual thoughts:
If you dream of a man, he is said to be a male ghost;
If you dream of a woman, she is a female ghost;
If you dream of animals, they are regarded as nagas;
If your dream is happy, you feel exalted;
If your dream is unhappy, you feel unhappy.
If you do not realise that ghosts arise from the root of mind,
You will not exhaust the ghosts of discursive thought.
Self-liberating good and evil is the meaning of this teaching.
This we call the oral instructions of dreams.
Lotsawa, have you realised their nature?

In the period between falling asleep and dreaming,
In that state of delusion, which is the essence of dharmakaya,
Inexpressible bliss and luminosity are experienced.
Then, seal that with luminosity
And the deep sleep of luminosity occurs.
This we call the oral instructions of luminosity.
Lotsawa, have you realised mind as unborn?

The eight doorways are the openings of samsara.
The one doorway is the path of mahamudra.
When the eight doorways are closed and the one doorway is

opened,
With the bow of prana, the arrow of mind
Is propelled by the bowstring HIK
And so consciousness is shot through the aperture of Brahma.
This we call the oral instructions of the ejection of consciousness.
Lotsawa, can you stop your prana at the right time?

When the time to leave the body comes,
One finds another body as an authentic sacred object.
Then the seed syllable rides the horse of prana.
By means of the wheels of prana,
One abandons one's body like an empty house
And enters the other body, which is the essence of nirmanakaya.
This we call the oral instructions of the transference of
consciousness.
Lotsawa, is your prana workable?

The mind at the time of dreaming
Should be mixed with the mind of bardo.
Its essence is sambhogakaya.
Both the pure and impure aspects of the two kayas of form
Are attained when the time of the bardo comes.
The pith of dream bardo is the mixing and ejecting of consciousness.
This we call the oral instructions of bardo.
Lotsawa, are you trained in the bardo?

It is necessary to study the outer and inner teachings.
Comprehending them will enable you to overcome the two
extremes.

When uncertainty as to existence and non-existence is cut,
That is the one path from which one does not stray.
On this path, how could there be sadness?

Another incident happened during this period. Marpa was learning the bathing yoga from Naropa one day. As he entered the pool possessing eight qualities, he set his yantra that was given to him by Naropa, down on the bank. That very moment, a crow came and flew away with it. But Naropa immediately realised that it was another act of the obstacles of Mara and he was able to paralyse the crow, by his yogic gaze. Returning the yantra to Marpa, Naropa said, "From now on, you will forever be victorious against the obstacles of Mara."

Finally, Naropa declared Marpa to be his regent. Marpa then asked Naropa to guide him as to the way in which this lineage was to progress in the event his own family line was cut. Naropa sadly informed him that his family lineage would go no further in the future, though he insisted that father and son should still practise the sadhanas of divine yidams in strict retreats. Naropa then explained that it was for this very purpose of taming students in Tibet that he had installed Marpa as his regent.

Naropa then placed his hand on Marpa's head and sang:

Possessing the karma of proper training in previous lives,
You are a yogin who has realised the innate truth.
You, Marpa the Translator from Tibet,
Are a bird of the five families soaring in the space of dharmata.
You will hold the royal treasures of a universal monarch.

The sky flower of your family lineage will vanish,
But your Dharma lineage will flow on like a wide river.
Though your desires appear vivid, like a carving in rock,
The ripples of samsara's waters will vanish by themselves.
Your sons will be like the children of lions and garudas.
Later disciples will be even better than the previous ones.
Having realised the meaning of the mahayana,
Those of good karma will be ripened and freed.
You are the king of those worthy students.

Now depart to U in Tibet.
In the Northern Land of Snow,
A place abundant with a variety of fragrant trees,
On a mountain slope blooming with various herbs,
Is a fortunate disciple who is a worthy vessel.
Son, go there and perform benefit for others.
You will certainly accomplish this benefit.

Because of our love, yearning, and intimacy in this life,
In the realm of luminosity we transcend meeting and parting.
In the next life, in the completely pure celestial realm,
I will receive you.
There is no doubt that we will be inseparable companions.
Son, rest your mind in this.

As the song came to an end, Naropa instructed Marpa to return to Maitripa once more and ask him about the teachings he wanted to learn. He declared that Marpa's understanding would now be deeper than before.

Going Home

Finally it was time for Marpa to leave for Tibet. His heart wreathed now that he had to leave his guru Naropa and his dharma brothers and sisters. Also, the perilous journey that lay ahead too scared him. But with all that he had learnt from his great guru this time, Marpa felt very proud about returning home. He thought, "In this life, I have come three times to India from Tibet; the first time for twelve years, the second time for six years and this time for three years. Twenty-one years have passed, and I have stayed for sixteen years and seven months before glorious Naropa. I have practiced the Dharma and have met with siddha gurus. I realise that I have completed my education in language and learning."

Marpa organised a ganacakra for Mahapandit Naropa. There, as the two gurus kept talking to each other, Marpa sang the grand song known as 'Long Song of the Journey'.

He sang:

Lord, kind leader of beings,
Gurus of the siddha lineage,

Please dwell as ornaments on the top of my head.
Dwelling there, please bless me.

Both Mahapandit Naropa of India
And Marpa the Translator from Tibet
Met because of previous practice and the same aspiration.
I attended you for sixteen years and seven months.
I accompanied you; we were not separate for an instant.
Therefore it is impossible for me not to be in your mind.

At this glorious monastery of Ravishing Beautiful Flowers,
You completely empowered me by the river of the four
abhishekas.
You gave me the ultimate oral instructions of the hearing lineage.
In the non-dual truth of the supreme, unsurpassable vehicle,
I meditated one-pointedly
And grabbed the sunyata-mind.
For the Northern Land of Snow,
You established me as regent and prophesied.
Therefore I, a novice, now go to Tibet.

As for me, a novice, going to Tibet:
There are three things I miss upon leaving.
There are three things that make me sad.
There are three things I fear on the road.
There are three things I am apprehensive of on the way.
There are three things ahead that make me proud.
There are three great wonders.
If I do not interpret this song,

The words and their meaning will not coincide.

As for the three things I miss upon leaving:
Headed by Lord Naropa and Maitripa,
There are a hundred siddha gurus.
Leaving them behind, I miss them more than my mother.

Headed by Sri Abhayakirti,
There are a hundred dharma brothers and sisters.
Leaving them behind, I miss them more than my mother.

Headed by the place Pullahari,
There are a hundred holy places of siddhas.
Leaving them behind, I miss them more than my mother.

As for the three things that make me sad:
Divine Dharmabodhi Asoka and others
Were my kind hosts and hostesses.
Not daring to separate from them, I feel sad.

The brahmin youth Suvarnamala,
Dead or alive, will always be my friend.
Not daring to separate from him, I feel sad.

The dark-skinned daughter of the merchant
Was with me constantly as an authentic consort.
Not daring to separate from her, I feel sad.

As for the three things I fear on the road:

The foremost is the boiling poison lake,
But soon I have to cross the Ganges river in the East.
Even before I see this, I am afraid.

In the jungle of the Usiri mountain,
Bandits and thieves lie in wait on the road.
Even before I see them, I am afraid.

At a city in Tirahuti,
Shameless custom taxes fall like rain.
Even before I see them, I am afraid.

As for the three things I am apprehensive of on the way
Not only is there the dangerous defile of Palahati,
There are eighty-one dangerous bridges and passages.
Kye ma! I quake like quicksilver.

Not only is there the snow pass of Khala Chela,
There are eighty-one small and large passes.
Kye ma! I quake like quicksilver.

Not only is there the great plain Paimo Palthang,
There are eighty-one small and large plains.
Kye ma! I quake like quicksilver.

As for the three things ahead that make me proud:
Headed by the grammars of Kalapa and Candra,
I know one hundred and eight different languages.
In the company of fellow translators, I will feel proud.

Headed by the Catuhpitha and the Hevajra,
I know one hundred and eight commentaries on the tantras.
In the company of fellow great teachers, I will feel proud.

Headed by the oral instructions of the four special transmissions,
I know one hundred and eight hearing lineage teachings.
In the company of fellow meditators, I will feel proud.

As for the three great wonders:
Besides the mixing of mind and prana, and the ejecting of consciousness,
I know one hundred and eight special dharmas.
O how wondrous, how great indeed!

Besides the devi Vetali,
I know one hundred and eight protectors of the teachings.
O how wondrous, how great indeed!

Besides the oral guidance in the five stages,
I know one hundred and eight sampannakramas.
O how wondrous, how great indeed!

All these are the kindness of the lord guru.
Even though I cannot repay his kindness,
Still the lord dwells inseparably as an ornament on the top of my head.

Finally, I, a novice, going to Tibet,
Request from my dharma brothers and sisters

Good wishes that my journey be free from obstacles.

This is the last time we will ever meet.
Let us definitely meet in the next life
In the celestial realm of glorious Uddiyana.

At the end of the song, Marpa learnt the four abhishekas of the body mandala of the guru; he prayed with him and finally left him for the last time. His dharma brothers and sisters escorted him for a while. Marpa kept walking backwards all the way till he reached the bottom of the stone steps of Pullahari. He prostrated before his guru for one last time. The footprint that he left there can still be seen today.

Naropa and the dakinis blessed Marpa so that he could reach home safely. Then the dakinis took Naropa with them to the celestial realm in that very life. Marpa was now confident that he would surely benefit the sentient beings in Tibet till the end of his life.

As per Naropa's instructions, Marpa first went and stayed with Maitripa for a while. There he once again learnt the abhishekas of Hevajra. While he was learning these instructions, a rain of divine flowers started to fall from the sky. Marpa knew that was a sign from the dakinis, expressing that they had accepted him. Marpa now came to the conclusion that both Maitripa and Naropa were indeed even greater than the Buddha.

The Final Years

Marpa finally returned to Tibet. He carried out the divine teachings of Naropa and tried to instil Dharma in the hearts of the people back at home. He travelled far and wide and everywhere the people welcomed him warmly. Marpa's fame spread far and wide.

Often he would be heard singing this song:

Blessed by the glorious and venerable Hermit
Who has completely mastered the ultimate wisdom, the essential
truth,
The pith instructions of the Dharma of Mahamudra,
Great lord Master, I pay homage to you.
Vajra brothers and sisters, my heart friends,
We cannot be separated by any means.
Brothers and sisters, though our bodies are separate,
Our minds are one.
Are you not the glorious Abhayakirti?
I, who came from the land of India,
And you, who dwell in central Nepal,

*Since the conditions for our long lives have not waned in
strength,*
Now on this holy day
At this ganacakra of the dakinis,
We meet together again.
It must be that there is no hypocrisy in our samaya.
I feel completely joyful.
Do you, who are sitting here, feel joyful too?
Though I am a stupid novice from Tibet,
You call me the famous translator.
You said, "Translator, sing a Tibetan song."
Though my voice is not good,
I cannot refuse your request, honourable ones.
Here is a song recalling the kindness
Of both Lord Naropa and Maitripa.
There are various ways of seeing their wonders.
Listen carefully, brothers and sisters!
The realised Lord Maitripa
Is famed far and wide
As a Nirmanakaya who lives in India.
In a city in the valley of Vaishali,
The king, the protector of the earth, attended the lord,
Touching his crown
To the anthers of the lord's lotus feet
Among the mahapandits of the five sciences
Maitripa is known as the Master, the crest jewel
The banner of his fame is renowned in the ten directions
In the month of miracles of the Bird year,
Through his mastery in making offerings to the Sugata,

His name became universally renowned as the Master.
This lord Buddha gave the transmission
Of the perfection of the yanas, the pith instructions,
The Dharma of Mahamudra:
"Outer grasping, the appearance of sense objects,
Continuously flows as great bliss.
Realise it as unborn Dharmakaya.
"Inner fixation, the mind-consciousness
Is discursive, which cannot be grasped as real.
Therefore, see it as naked insight without foundation.
"Generally, all dharmas of apparent existence
Are primordially non-existent and unborn.
Realise them as the essence of simplicity.
"Do not desire to abandon samsara
And there is no nirvana to attain.
Samsara and nirvana are the self-liberated innate state.
Realise this unity as great bliss.
"Even if you emptied out the minds of the Buddhas of the three times,
There is nothing more ultimate than this," Maitripa sang.
I have cut all doubts with this.
This is the approach of the great Lord Maitripa.
If you express the view, do it this way.
I present this offering song to the three jewels.
May it gladden the hearts of you sitting here.

Through these songs, Marpa warmed the hearts of all the people who had gathered before him to listen to his teachings.

Again, whenever people would talk to him about Naropa and
ask him about the experience that he had with the Mahapandit,
Marpa would say:

I prostrate to the lord siddhas.
Grant your blessings to me, a fortunate one.
Guide me, your yearning son, on the path.
Though I have no skill in singing,
I cannot refuse your request, my honourable dharma brothers
and sisters.
Now I will sing this song of pride untouched even by death.
You, who are assembled here, take this to heart
And practice the Dharma properly.
I, Marpa the Translator from Tibet,
And Mahapandit Naropa of India
Met in a city in a valley blooming with flowers,
At the mountain monastery of the Golden Land.
This seemed to be the result of pure aspiration in former lives
At this famous and blessed place,
I attended the renowned jetsun
For sixteen years and seven months.
I received the full four abhishekas seven times.
He granted me the blessing of Sri Cakrasamvara.
He taught me the profound Tantra of Hevajra.
He gave me the yidam, the co-emergent consort.
Again and again, I requested oral instructions.
I grabbed the path of the nadis and prana,
And Buddha was in the palm of my hand.
One day, when so-called death is revealed,

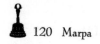

I will be freed from the trap of my inherited body,
I will have the confidence of the profound teachings on the moment of death,
I will join the techniques of mixing and ejecting,
And I will be received by dakas and dakinis.
Accompanied by the victory banners and symphony of music,
I will go to the celestial realm of great bliss.
There I am certain to meet glorious Naropa.
Now, even if I die, I feel proud.
All you lords and trantikas sitting here,
If you do not receive the transmission of the hearing lineage,
Do not hope to attain the enlightenment in one lifetime.
Through the sophistry of the scholastic lineage.
However, if you intend to practice the holy Dharma wholeheartedly,
Take hold of the lineage of Naropa and Maitripa.
Later disciples will be even better than previous ones.
They go from bliss to bliss.
Did my song agree with you, you who are sitting here?
Please forgive me if the meaning is confused.

The people present before Marpa would also ask him about the various other gurus that he had met in India and what he learnt from them. To those questions, Marpa would say:

Successor of the Great Brahmin,
He has realised the innate truth free from extremes,
And is therefore the yogin of space, beyond analogy.
His name is renowned as Maitripa.

I am a follower of the tradition of this father jetsun.
He is a yogin for whom meditation is inseparable from the path.
This Marpa the Translator
Was born in an inferior place, but the place he visited is supreme.
I went to India three times,
Without consideration for life and limb, I sought the holy Dharma.
I met the lord Nirmanakaya Buddhas.
Who accepted me with the abhishekas along with their oral instructions
Now I will repay their kindness.
You asked me, "How many gurus do you have?"
I am linked with thirteen gurus by dharmic aspiration.
In particular, there are five siddhas.
Among them, there are two lords unrivalled by anyone,
Chiefly, Mahapandit Naropa.
And after him, Prince Maitripa.
The kindness of Maitripa is even greater than a mother's.
Missing him more and more,
I went to the Ganges river in the East.
At the monastery of Blazing fire Mountain,
In the cool shade of a nyagrodha tree,
I saw the great lord Master sitting there.
Joy like that of the first bhumi arose.
I presented an offering to please the guru,
I set out flowers of pure gold.
I joined my palms and offered a full prostration
Longing with one-pointed mind, I supplicated him.

I requested the profound Tantra Manjushri-nama sangiti,
And the yidam Hevajra.
He gave me the ultimate Mahamudra.
He is Sri Advaya Avadhuti
Thus the father jetsun kindly accepted me,
He empowered me with the four profound inner sign abhishekas.
He blessed me, completely purifying my being.
The germ of motivation sprouted deep within.
Inwardly, the character of insight-mind
Is luminosity, free from arising and ceasing.
Thus he showed me the unfabricated, innate essence.
Momentary thoughts dissolved into space
And undefiled bliss arose within.
The stream of alaya, primordially pure,
Was resolved as the ground of trikaya.
I met mind as mother dharmata, face to face.
At that time, there were wondrous signs:
A cedar torch the size of a finger's length
Burned for seven days.
A tree, though inanimate,
Became unbearably agitated and moved.
There emanated seven red jackals
Whom I actually saw receive torma.
Dakinis dwelling at the three levels,
Though invisible, proclaimed the sounds of mantras.
Ksetrapalas filled the sky,
And I heard the sounds of various musical instruments.
" After three births,

You will attain the supreme siddhi,"
Thus I heard from the great lord Master.
Even though I am unworthy, my guru is good.
Thus, I solved the final point of the view of Dharma
And have no fear of falling into inferior views.
This is the approach of the great Lord Maitripa.
Gladden your hearts and practice in this way.

People would be overjoyed to hear these songs.

Marpa practiced according to the oral instructions that he received, and excellent experiences and realisations were born in his heart. In particular, Marpa attained confidence through practising the transference of consciousness.

Once some disciples, headed by Gyang-ro Shangton were offering a thanksgiving ganacakra. At that time, a pigeon was flying behind its mother, pursued by a hawk. Though the young pigeon escaped to its nest, it died from being out of breath.

Seeing its corpse, Marpa said, "I will show you a demonstration of the transference of consciousness today." He tied a string to the pigeon's leg and then transferred his consciousness. The pigeon arose, and slowly flew up to reunite affectionately with its mother.

Gyang-ro Shangton looked at the guru's body. It had the appearance of a corpse and he became terrified. Weeping before the body, he requested, "Precious guru, please do not do this." As this had no effect, he became even more frightened. Then he

Marpa was a master of transference of consciousness.

went before the pigeon and supplicated.

The pigeon fell over and immediately the guru arose, and said:

Having abandoned my body like an empty house,
I entered another body, a young pigeon.
Extending its wings and about to fly in the sky,
The mother and son birds met affectionately.
Everyone witnessed this; what a great wonder!

Then Marpa sang this song of the greatness of the secret mantra:

I, Marpa Lotsawa,
Know the king of tantras, the Hevajra.
I have the oral instructions of Mahapandit Naropa.
If I do not remain in solitude, it is a disservice to myself.
I know the king of tantras, the Catuhpitha.
I have the oral instructions of the ejection and transference of
consciousness.
If I die in the ordinary way, it is a disservice to myself.

I know how to mix dhyana and sleep.
I have the oral instructions of the luminosity of dreams.
If I sleep in the ordinary way, it is a disservice to myself.
I know the candali, the regal way of holding the mind.
I have the oral instructions that pierce to the pith of mind.
If I do not practice their meaning, it is a disservice to myself.

I know the seventy qualities of prana.

I have the oral instructions of utilizing illness.
If I summon a doctor, it is a disservice to myself.

I know my body to be the mandala of the victorious ones.
If I do not expand nadi, prana, and bindu
Through enjoying meat and liquor, it is a disservice to myself.

In order to bring another person on the path,
I have the oral instructions of karmamudra.
If I do not enjoy the mudra, it is a disservice to myself.

Because he achieved certainty in the transference of consciousness, Marpa became completely renowned as a siddha, undisputed by anyone. In the same way, he gave the supreme single transmission lineage of the profound instructions on the transference of consciousness to his son Dharma Dode.

Sadly though, as predicted by Naropa, Marpa's son, who had mastered most of the oral instructions that his father had given down to him, died young. Even though father and son had gone away to a retreat to carry on with their studies, one day, Dharma Dode went to the village fair as the honourable guest. Though he should not have gone in the first place, his mother let him go there, after exacting some vows from him. But Dharma Dode got so busy with worldly pleasures that he soon forgot all about the promises that he had made to his mother. While he rode back home, on a horse, he met with an accident and his head was smashed.

When all the students and son-disciples gathered at a memorial service for Dharma Dode, they requested, "Precious guru, since your son is no more and you are now getting old, please prophesy how the precious teachings of the Kagyu will spread and how further disciples and actions will arise."

The guru said, "As a descendant of the lineage of Mahapandit Naropa, I have mastered recognising auspicious coincidence. Mahapandit Naropa gave excellent prophecies for the teachings of the Kagyu. Therefore, you great son-disciples should await your dreams."

After practising dream yoga, the great son-disciples related their dreams. Most of the dreams were rather good, but they were not prophetic. However, Jetsun Mila had a dream of four great pillars, which he offered to the guru as follows:

In accordance with the command of Lord Vajradhara,

Last night's dream
I will offer to the guru just as it occurred.
Please listen to me for a little while.
In this vast Northern region of Jambudvipa,
I dreamt that there was a massive snow mountain.
I dreamt that the snowy summit touched the skies.
I dreamt that the sun and moon circled around the peak.
I dreamt that their light rays filled the sky.
I dreamt that the base covered the vast ground.
I dreamt that rivers descended in the four directions.
I dreamt that their water satisfied all beings.

I dreamt that the rivers flowed into the ocean.
I dreamt that various flowers bloomed.
In general, I dreamt a dream like this.
Thus I relate it to you, guru, the buddha of the three times.

In particular, next to this massive, high snow mountain:
I dreamt that a great pillar was established in the East.
I dreamt that on top of the pillar a great lion was poised.
I dreamt that the lion was fully displaying his thick turquoise
mane.
I dreamt that his four paws clawed at the snow.
I dreamt that his eyes gazed upward.
I dreamt that the lion leapt to a white snow mountain range.
Thus I relate it to you, guru, the buddha of the three times.

I dreamt that a great pillar was established in the South.
I dreamt that on top of the pillar a tigress roared.
I dreamt that the tigress was fully displaying her well-striped
coat.
I dreamt that she puffed out her chest three times.
I dreamt that her four paws clawed at the jungle.
I dreamt that her eyes gazed upward.
I dreamt that the tigress leapt into a jungle.
I dreamt that she strode among the trees.
Thus I relate it to you, guru, the buddha of the three times.

I dreamt that a great pillar was established in the West.
I dreamt that above the pillar there soared a great garuda.
I dreamt that the garuda's wings were fully extended.

I dreamt that the horns of the garuda pointed to the sky.
I dreamt that his eyes gazed upward.
I dreamt that the garuda soared through the expanse of space.
Thus I relate it to you, guru, the buddha of the three times.

I dreamt that a great pillar was established in the North.
I dreamt that above the pillar there soared a great vulture.
I dreamt that the vulture's wings were fully extended.
I dreamt that the vulture made her nest among the rocks.
I dreamt that this vulture gave birth to a young one.
I dreamt that from this one the sky was filled with a flock of birds.
I dreamt that the vulture's eyes gazed upward.
I dreamt that the vulture soared through the expanse of space.
Thus I relate it to you, guru, the buddha of the three times.

Because of the auspicious coincidence of a dream like this,
I thought these might be good and virtuous signs.
I rejoiced and felt inspired.
Please interpret this and grant us a prophecy.

Marpa was very pleased and said, "This is an excellent dream."
He told his wife Dagmema to prepare a good ganacakra.

When his wife had gathered the requisites together and the great son-disciples had assembled, they performed a splendid ganacakra. The guru said, "Mila Dorje Gyaltsen has had an excellent dream. O how wondrous indeed!"

Finally, towards the end of his life, Marpa decided to pass on his lineage to Milarepa. It was Milarepa then who was responsible for the sun of the Buddha's teachings rising in the snowy mountain peaks of Tibet. The dark ignorance of all sentient beings was finally dispelled.

Teachings of Marpa

Song 1

Leader, glorious Kanakasri,
Brothers and sisters sitting here, listen to me!
If you ask who I am,
I am the famed Marpa the Translator.
My umbilical cord was cut in U in the land of Tibet.
I was educated in Southern Nepal and India.
I travelled to India three times.
This last time, I truly made persistent request.
Touching their lotus feet to my head,
My gurus bestowed on me the amrta of true speech.
Generally, I have many gurus with whom I have a dharmic
connection.
Led by glorious Simhadvipa,
They have completely mastered insight and the higher
perceptions,
And thirteen of them can transform one's perception of the
world.
Amongst all of them, the most worthy of offering

Is the unrivalled Lord Naropa,
Who is great Vajradhara in human form.
There is no way to repay this lord's kindness.
Though deeply missing the father Nirmanakaya,
I could not find him anywhere.
Whatever face I saw, it was not his.
Finally, in the foothills of Dark Forest mountain,
I saw on a boulder of wondrous crystal,
Like a symbol carved in relief,
Footprints left by the father jetsun.
O how wondrous, how great indeed!
Above a medicinal sandalwood tree,
Through a miraculous display of Naropa's compassion,
The nine emanation devis of the Hevajra mandala appeared.
In the heart center of the coemergent consort,
The astamantra wheel
Appeared as if drawn with the tip of one hair,
With a variety of light rays streaming forth.
Thus, Naropa granted me the permission-blessing.
O wondrous, how great indeed!
Helplessly, I burst into tears.
Filled with yearning, I felt like crying forever.
Overwhelmed completely, I wailed aloud.
I supplicated him with one-pointed mind.
He looked on me with compassion and came before me.
Joy arose in me, like on the path of seeing.
O how wondrous, how great indeed!
I offered rare and precious gold dust.
He said, I do not want that

Again and again, I asked him to accept.
He said: Offer it to the father gurus and the three jewels,
And casually tossed it into the forest.
I was stunned with loss.
Saying, If you want it, here it is again
He opened his joined palms.
Not lost, unspoiled, it was there just as before.
O how wondrous, how great indeed!
Striking his big toe on the ground,
Rocks and pebbles became gold.
He said Everything is a land of gold
O how wondrous, how great indeed!
He gazed into the sky,
And from the stomach of a white-bellied fish,
He set out the offerings of a ganacakra
With food of a hundred flavours.
O how wondrous, how great indeed!
As I bathed in a pool of eight qualities,
A crow snatched away my protection yantra.
Naropa made the threatening yogic gaze and mudra,
At that very moment, the crow was paralyed and fell to the
earth.
Naropa said, You are victorious over the obstacles of Mara!
Oh how wondrous, how great indeed!
You should not stay here, but to go to Tibet.
In that Northern Land of Snow
Is a disciple who is worthy vessel
Thus, he gave this prophecy to me.
O how wondrous, how great indeed!

These are the eight wonders I saw
Of the Nirmanakaya, Mahapandit Naropa.
Besides you vajra brothers and sisters,
If I repeated this to anyone, they would not believe it.
In this dark age of the teaching,
People with perverted views and great envy
Will slander you if you speak of virtue.
Therefore, please keep this secret
And do not discuss these words with others besides yourselves.
I present this song of offering to the lord guru.
May it gladden your minds, my heart friends.

Song 2

Lord Aksobya, mahasukhakaya,
United with Vajradakini,
Chief of Dakas,
Sri Heruka, I praise you and prostrate.
Collector of all commands and secret mantras,
Possessor of the Secret,
Propagator of the holy Dharma in the world of men,
Lord Nagarjuna, father and son, I praise you.
You who bring down the overwhelming vajra thunderbolt,
The kind one who protects from fear,
Tilopa, lord of the three levels,
Who has attained supreme siddha, I praise you.
Undergoing twelve trials attending the guru,
All the pitakas and tantras,

You realised in an instant;
Lord Buddha in human form, I praise you.
Indestructible form of Mahamudra,
Possessing the uncontrived primordial essence,
Realising the truth of the bliss of simplicity,
Lord Prince Maitripa, I praise you.
Expounding the doctrine of the command lineage,
Attaining the siddha of profound Guhyasamaja,
You are endowed with compassion and wisdom,
Venerable Jnanagharbha, I praise you.
Dwelling in charnel grounds, solitudes and under trees,
A Kusulu savouring potency,
Possessing the miracle of travelling in space,
Kukuripa, I praise you.
Having realised the truth of abundance,
Possessing the potency of moonbeams,
You satisfy and bring bliss to those who see you,
Yogini, I praise you.
Resting in the shade of the excellent umbrella,
Adorned with golden ribbons,
Seated in the sky, attaining mastery over the sun and moon,
Jetsun of Nepal, I praise you.
Overcoming the worldly attachment of grasping and fixation,
Possessing the benefit of attending the guru,
Holding principally to the practice of enlightenment,
Preserving the learning of Mahayana,
Clearing away obstructions as well as obstacles caused by agents
of perversion,
The friend who introduces one to the good guru,

Guiding masters, I praise you.
The merit of praising the guru,
Is equal to that of offering to the Buddhas of the three times.
By this merit of praising the masters,
May all beings attend spiritual friends.

Song 3

Blessed by the lord forefathers,
I am a translator from Tibet.
Born on the border of Mön and Tibet,
My karmic connection was reawakened in the place of
Mangkhar.
From the translator Drogmi
I learned the colloquial and literary languages and grammars.
I sought the holy Dharma in the land of India.
With a gait like a wheel of wind
I travelled from the land of Tibet.
The Buddha, Mahapandit Naropa,
And I, Marpa the Translator of Tibet,
Met as Buddha and sentient being.
I received the full abhishekas seven times.
Overall I have thirteen gurus.
Naropa and Maitripa are like the sun and moon;
Mahapandit Naropa is the chief one.
I saw great wonders like these:
Above a medicinal sandalwood tree
I saw the nine emanation devis of Hevajra.
In the heart centre of coemergent consort

I saw the astamantra wheel.
From the stomach of a white-bellied fish
I received food of a hundred flavours.
Thus I saw the self-born Sambhogakaya
I saw the inner mind as Dharmakaya.
I saw the outer appearances as Nirmanakaya.
Emanations of Buddha Naropa
I saw filling all space.
In natural boulder of crystal
I saw the footprint left by Naropa.
There is no greater wonder than this.
When the Master, Prince Maitripa,
Gave abhishekas in the forest,
I saw jackals roaming in the cemetery
Actually receiving the torma.
I saw the dakinis of the three levels.
Actually performing their activities.
This illusory contrivance of outer appearance
Was locked in the house of still space.
Appearance, this dream of habitual patterns,
Dissolved and disappeared into luminosity.
A cedar torch a finger's length in size
Burned for seven days.
I touched the feet of the great Maitripa,
The yogin for whom meditation is inseparable from the path.
I hold the lineage of the great Brahmin.
I saw great wonders like these.
If I explain all of my realisation,
Some of you will not be able to contain it in your mind.

If I explain just a corner of it, it is like this:
Having confidence in luminosity
Is indeed the view free form bias or partiality.
Meditation is continuous, like flowing of a wide river.
By not regarding meditation as limited to the four periods
And by abandoning hypocritical thoughts,
There is no distinction between meditation and post meditation.
By obtaining the power of both prana and mind,
The fear of samsara disappeared long ago.
These are my realisations.

Song 4

Lord who has realised the essential truth,
The dharmakaya,
Your name is renowned as Maitripa.
When I think of you and your kindness,
I miss you greatly.
I continually yearn one-pointedly for you.
Father nirmanakaya, grant your blessings.
You, kind guru, are the guide
Headed by Sri Paindapa,
You yogins and yoginis sitting here,
Listen a while to this song.
This song possesses the blessings of the dakinis.
I, the teacher Marpa Chokyi Lodro,
Spent one-third of my life in India.
For forty years, I have learned and studied.
Last year, the dangerous Snake year,

In the Hawk month of miracles,
I was on the road.
I crossed the terrifying river Ganges.
Two low-caste bandits, happy to die,
Dove into the water like fish,
And raced toward me like horses across a plain.
Thinking of past and future lives, I panicked.
I meditated on the Father jetsun on the top of my head.
They looked at me again and again, stopped and turned around.
Like rescuing a drowning man, his kindness saved my life.
Father, it is impossible to repay your kindness.
In the first part of last month,
On the tenth day of the waxing of the moon,
At the Ramadoli charnel ground,
I presented offerings to please the gurus.
I conducted a ganacakra to please the dakinis.
When I saw the yogins assembled there,
I suddenly recalled Lord Naropa and Maitripa.
Inseparable from their loving kindness, I am protected.
Therefore, I called to mind the actions of the father.
Overwhelmed with yearning, I burst into tears.
Then I thought, Should I return to India again?
In a dream at the break of day,
A woman dressed in clothes made of leaves
Stretched out her right hand
And touched my head with her fingers,
Saying, You should not return to India,
But to go to U in the land of Tibet.
You will arrive in the Land of Snow

Without any outer or inner obstacles arising.
There are students there who are worthy vessels.
She gave me this blessing and prophecy.
Surely, she was a ksetrapala dakini.
Then, through the kindness of the jetsun,
Last night, after my dreams born from habitual patterns,
I saw the lord Master, Prince Maitripa,
Travelling through the sky riding a lion.
He arrived in front of me
And showed three signs revealing the unborn.
He spoke the Dharma without letter,
I realised an inexpressible truth.
An unprecedented experience dawned.
At daybreak, as soon as I woke up,
I remembered Lord Maitripa again and again.
I could not separate him from my mind.
I wailed and cried, covering my face with tears.
I could not breathe, my lungs were blocked,
Father, in my heart, I long for you, like thirsty man for water.
Do you know of my longing?
Father, nirmanakaya, guide me on the path.
Although generally dreams are born form habitual patterns,
The father jetsun appeared, O wondrous, how great indeed!
The greatest joy and deepest sorrow arose.
You are sitting here, this is what I say to you.

Song 5

Lord Paindapa, you who practice yogic discipline!
Your name had been prophesised by the devas; O how
wondrous, how great indeed!
Under the hand of glorious Advayalalita
Are the vajra brothers and sisters, whose minds do not differ.
Headed by Sri Gunamati,
Dakas, who are sitting in the right hand row, listen to me!
After them the secret yoginis,
Headed by the consort Sukhavajri,
Dakinis who are sitting in the left hand row, listen to me!
Generally, all dharmas are illusion.
Dreams are exalted as special illusion.
Early in the night, dreams arise born from habitual patterns.
There is nothing whatsoever to rely on there.
At midnight, the deceptions of Mara appear.
One should not trust in these.
At dawn, there are prophecies by the devas.
O how wondrous, how great indeed!
At the break of dawn this morning,
The great lord Master appeared.
And taught the Dharma which revealed the ultimate.
This is the unforgettable memory of what Maitripa said:
In general, all dharmas are mind.
The guru arises from one's mind.
There is nothing other than mind.
Everything that appears is the nature of mind.
Which is primordially nonexistent.
The natural state, unborn and innate,

Cannot be abandoned by the effort of thought.
So rest at ease, naturally, without restriction.
This can be shown by signs:
A human corpse, an outcaste, a dog, a pig,
An infant, a madman, an elephant,
A precious jewel, a blue lotus,
Quicksilver, a deer, a lion,
A Brahmin, and a black antelope; did you see them?
Maitripa said.
The realisation of the truth was shown by these signs:
Not fixated on either samsara or nirvana,
Not holding acceptance or rejection in one's being,
Not hoping for fruition from others,
Mind free from occupation and complexity,
Not falling into four extremes,
Nonmeditation and nonwandering,
Free from thought and speech,
Beyond any analogy whatsoever.
Through the kindness of the guru, I realised these.
Since the experience of these realisations has dawned,
Mind and mental events have ceased,
And space and insight are inseperable.
Faults and virtues neither increase nor decrease.
Bliss, emptiness and luminosity are unceasing.
Therefore, luminosity dawns beyond coming or going.
This transmission of the innate, the pith of the view,
Through the sign meanings which reveal the unborn,
I heard from the great lord Master.
The reason why I sing these words

Is the insistent request of the honourable lord.
I could not refuse the dharma brothers and sisters.
Dakinis, do not be jealous!

Song 6

As for that which is called a ganacakra:
When one performs the four abhishekas, the path that ripens,
A ganacakra is necessary.
When one performs consecration,
A ganacakra is necessary.
When one requests the blessings of the dakinis,
A ganacakra is necessary.
When there is teaching of and listening to the tantras,
A ganacakra is necessary.
When one requests profound oral instructions,
A ganacakra is necessary.
This Marpa the Translator
Has gone to India three times.
In general, ganacakras are inconceivable.
In particular, I have seen great wonders like these:
To the Mahapandit Jetsun Naropa,
A royal sovereign ruler
And Kundali, the daughter of a tavern owner,
Made an offering of karsapana coins
Arranged on a mandala of precious bell metal.
They had supplicated a year in advance
And great Lord Naropa had accepted.
Then at a charnel ground in a teak forest,

Naropa performed a ganacakra three times.
With immeasurable wealth and enjoyments,
Elaborate feast offerings and torma were arranged.
By the blessing of glorious Naropa,
The divine assembly of Sri Cakrasamvara,
An equal number of yogins and yoginis of the secret mantra,
Altogether sixty-two women-
Conversed in profound code language.
Emanating from the heart center of the great Lord Naropa,
The divine assembly of Cakrasamvara,
Resided splendidly in the center of the mandala.
Performing the full sadhana,
The great Jetsun Naropa,
Held the vajra and ghanta in his hands,
And wore the six bone ornaments.
In space, a cubit above the ground,
He stood in the dance posture with his right leg extended.
The other yogins and yoginis
Sounded damarus with their right hands
And held cymbals in their left.
Thus I saw them enjoying and performing the dances.
I, Marpa the Translator,
Saw the co emergent dharmakaya,
The essence of the profound fourth abhishekas.
I met a lord like this.
I saw a ganacakra like this.
This is not for the ordinary, nor for the way of the ordinary.
Isn't this a great wonder, teacher of Tsang?

Song 7

Lord nirmanakaya who dwells in the land of India,
In the valley of Vaisali in Magadha,
You defeated the attacks of heretics
And were appointed the great guardian of the gate.
You are famed as Lord Naropa.
Father nirmanakaya, I pay homage at your feet.
At the palace in a city of outlaws in the East,
While I was looking through the profound Hevajra-tantra,
My mind was uncomfortable and agitated.
Though I drew it like a bow, it flew away like an arrow.
Suddenly, I remembered Mahapandit Naropa
And overwhelming yearning filled my mind.
I was looking for Naropa in a forest near the border
When, unknowingly, I was trapped in a town of barbarous
people.
Through his tyranny, the king held me in a prison.
In a palace heaped with glorious flowers,
I acted as the king's officiating priest for three days.
In the hearth of blazing fire offerings,
I saw whatever food and drink I desired miraculously arise.
I thought, O how wondrous, how great indeed!
I set out to search again.
I carried three measures of white rice for staple
And for meat a white-bellied fish.
Lord Paindapa who practices yogic discipline
Knew the land and so accompanied me as a guide.
For half a month I wandered in the four directions.
Roaming through the forests and charnel grounds.

I could not find the jetsun anywhere.
Though I did not find Mahapandit Naropa,
I saw signs of great wonder:
Above a medicinal sandalwood tree,
The nine emanation devis of Hevajra,
Almost touching the branches,
Appeared in the sphere of a rainbow.
A wondrous sign, how great indeed!
In the heart center of the coemergent consort,
The astamantra wheel,
Like a reflection in a mirror,
Clearly appeared, unobscured by her outer form.
A wondrous sign, how great indeed!
On a white crystal boulder,
A very hard and solid vajra rock,
I saw the footprint of great Lord Naropa,
Complete in detail with even the imprint of his hair.
A wondrous sign, how great indeed!
I thought, it won't be long now,
And supplicated for a week.
Since the father clearly knows the minds of others,
The jetsun arrived before me in person.
I cried and wept with great joy.
Lowering myself, I placed the soles of his feet on the top of my
head.
Wailing, I said, You have been so unkind.
My tears of longing flowed like blood.
A wondrous sign, how great indeed!
I embraced his body like a consort.

I touched my head to his heart.
At that time he bestowed the complete abhisheka on my mind,
Pouring the essence of mind into me, thus completing the
teachings.
A wondrous sign, how great indeed!
Generally, both Mahapandit Naropa of India
And I, the teacher Lodro, Marpa of Tibet,
Met as Buddha and sentient being.
There is no doubt that I will become a siddha.
A wondrous sign, how great indeed!
You who keep samaya are like my heart son.
Basically, when I went to India,
Whenever I felt poor in wealth and possessions,
I filled a bowl with precious gold.
Such a story is worthy of fame; O wondrous,
How great indeed!
Since you are not stingy with your wealth,
You collected the last of your shoes and clothing,
And sent me away with all that I needed.
This was burying treasure, provisions for your next life.
Again I thought, O wondrous, how great indeed!
The son's mind is more tender than the father's.
Isn't this you, Marpa Golek?
What need to speak of your generosity with illusory wealth?
Your way is not to be concerned with this life.
A wonder greater than this is impossible.
How could I forget this long journey?
In the forest of Lhokha at the border of Tibet and Nepal,
Even in winter at the New Year, a ridge blooms with flowers.

In that land where white salu rice is sown,
In that country of Mon where the language is different,
The heat makes it difficult to survive any sickness,
But I risked my life without fear of death.
Son, in order to keep the difficult samaya,
Keep this in mind; I, the father, won't forget this either.
At this time, it is certain that we will not meet in the next life.
In the presence of yidams and dakinis,
Let us, father and son, aspire together.
In order to express my gratitude for what you have done
I have sung this song for your benefit.
Please do not proclaim this to others; keep it a secret.
Now I have given you these teachings to repay your kindness.
Keep this confidential; we will speak of it privately.
We have met before and are the best of friends.
From now until we die, let us be together.

Song 8

Lord Vajradhara whose essence is Aksobhya,
Please dwell as the crest ornament on the crown of my head.
Once I relate the examples of my difficult labours,
You lords, great teachers staying here,
Should practice the Dharma properly, not regarding it as easy.
This Marpa the Translator
Was born in the center of Lhodrak.
My karmic connection to the white Dharma was reawakened.
At the glorious monastery in Nyugu valley,
Under the translator Drogmi Lotsawa.

I learned the colloquial and literary languages and grammars.
His kindness certainly is great, not small.
I sought the holy Dharma in the land of India.
While travelling the path in Nepal,
I crossed over endless precipices and rivers,
Went through endless thick forests,
And travelled a long, endless road.
I was alone, like a solitary tree or a human corpse.
Enduring all the suffering on this path,
Even the wings of a soaring bird would tremble.
Nevertheless, it was worth the price of such fatigue.
I saw Nepal, heaven descended on Earth.
Seeing such sense pleasures, one could never get enough.
I thought, this is a land of demigods in the desire realm.
This must be golden age.
Through the way was difficult to travel, it was best to keep going.
While going there to India,
In the barbarous regions I encountered bandits, happy to die.
There seemed no hope that my life would be saved.
When I heard the roars of the beasts of prey,
Little did I think that this body would reach a comfortable place.
When I saw the breath of a giant serpent,
Though my mind was steady, my steps faltered.
All these dangerous things, I saw upon the path.
Even remembering them now, my heart and lungs tremble.
Finally, I crossed the famous Ganges River.
Nevertheless, it was worth the price of such hardship.
I saw the magnificent sights of Magadha.
Beginning with glorious Vajrasana,

I made offerings to wondrous shrines.
I thought, I have arrived too late.
Anxiously, I searched for the Dharma with all my heart.
Like a river, I wandered East and West through the land of India.
On a plain so vast it was difficult to cross,
I thought, I have arrived on a plane of fire.
Though I thought of the Dharma, my heart swelled with
depression.
I was overcome by the heat and a fever, which made it difficult
to survive.
I came near to death thirteen times.
There was no one with whom to leave a will of three words.
Three times I passed into a coma.
Seeing all the suffering of that time,
Even hateful enemies should shed tears.
Nevertheless, it was worth the price of risking my life.
Headed by the lord, Mahapandit Naropa,
There were five siddha gurus I met.
In general, I studied the four orders of tantra.
In particular, I learned the complete mother tantra
As well as the Guhyasamaja of the father tantra.
I went to the bank of the river Ganges in the East.
By the blessings of Lord Maitripa,
I attained the realisation of the ground, unborn dharmata,
Grabbed the sunyata-mind,
Saw the innate essence, the truth of simplicity,
Met the mother trikaya in person,
And resolved my own complexity at the time.
When I returned again to U in the land of Tibet,

I thought, I have the greatest oral instructions.
I thought, some disciples will become siddhas.
I thought, Many benefits for beings have been accomplished.
These are my profound confidences
This is the way I endured hardship.
Think of how difficult it is to obtain the Dharma;
Please do not be lazy, but practice!

Song 9

I, Marpa Lotsawa,
Know the king of tantras, the Hevajra.
I have the oral instructions of Mahapandit Naropa.
If I do not remain in solitude, it is a disservice to myself.
I know the king of tantras, the Catuhpitha.
I have the oral instructions of the ejection and transference of
consciousness.
If I die in the ordinary way, it is a disservice to myself.
I know how to mix dhyana and sleep.
I have the oral instructions of the luminosity of dreams.
If I sleep in the ordinary way, it is a disservice to myself.
I know the candali, the regal way of holding the mind.
I have the oral instructions that pierce to the pith of mind.
If I do not practice their meaning, it is a disservice to myself.
I know the seventy qualities of prana.
I have the oral instructions of utilizing illness.
If I summon a doctor, it is a disservice to myself.
I know my body to be the mandala of the victorious ones.
If I do not expand nadi, prana, and bindu

Through enjoying meat and liquor, it is a disservice to myself.
In order to bring another person on the path,
I have the oral instructions of karmamudra.
If I do not enjoy the mudra, it is a disservice to myself.

Song 10

Bhagavat, great Vajradhara,
In this dark age of five thousand years,
When you ripen and free those of good karma
You appear in the form of the great Lord Naropa.
This unresourceful Marpa the Translator—
Do you hear, see, or think of him?
O father nirmanakaya, please accept me with kindness.
In the avadhuti, the main path of enlightenment,
Prana and mind, bliss and warmth are united,
Becoming unconditioned great bliss.
The wisdom ofunobscured insight dawns.
"This is unsurpassable," the guru has said.
The darkness of ignorance is purified in space.
One is free from the two obscurations of grasping and fixation.
Therefore bliss and luminosity dawn in simplicity.
This appearance of collective coincidence
Is a reflection without self-nature.
All appearances are realised like that,
And just like appearances in a dream,
All Dharmas arise as illusions.
Gods, asuras, humans,
Hell beings, pretas, animals—

These various ways of fixating on appearance
Are realised as nonexistent, like an illusion.
When conceptions of the world and its inhabitants
And the gate through which these arise are controlled by the
technique of prana,
There appears whatever is desired.
Therefore the mixing and ejecting of consciousness arise free
from stain.
When thoughts arise, rest naturally.
When dreaming, be mindful without corrupting it.
When in the bardo, don't control, but be aware.
When there is fruition, let it arise without obscuration.
You followers of Naropa,
Practice the profound oral instructions.
As you have insight, certainty will arise.
Narrow-minded people with perverse realisation
Slander even the Buddha.
Cursing even their own shadow,
They chase after deception
And cannot distinguish truth from falsity.
When the fool runs and cries out,
The wise do not follow.
The Dharma is empty of sophistry.
This body is a mandala of deities.
This speech is the nature of Dharma.
This mind is the essence of wisdom.
Sons, practice free from boredom.
Undoubtedly, you will attain enlightenment.

Song 11

I prostrate to the father gurus.
By the kindness of the lord forefathers,
When in solitude and at leisure, I meditate on nadi and prana.
Exerting body and mind again and again, I meditate.
Even when my elements are in turmoil, I have no anxiety.
I have confidence in knowing this will heighten my practice.
While asleep, I meditate on luminosity.
Focusing appearances again and again, I meditate.
Even when experiencing delusion, I have no anxiety.
I have confidence in knowing this as unity.
At the time of dream, I meditate on the illusory body.
Expanding on appearances again and again, I meditate.
Even when the dreams become discursive, I have no anxiety.
I have confidence in knowing them as illusory.
While enjoying sense pleasures, I meditate on the deity.
Experiencing their taste again and again, I meditate.
Even when seeing ordinary food and drink, I have no anxiety.
I have confidence in knowing these as a feast offering.
On the occasion of upayamarga, I meditate on another's body.
Arousing bliss again and again, I meditate.
Even when it appears to be mundane, I have no anxiety.
I have confidence in knowing this as coemergent.
At the time of death, I meditate on the ejection of
consciousness.
Practicing the ejection of consciousness again and again, I
meditate.
Even when the signs of death appear, I have no anxiety.
I have confidence in knowing them as sampannakrama.

At the time of death, I enter the bardo.
The bardo is like a cloud or mist.
Even when passion and aggression arise, I have no anxiety.
I have confidence in knowing them as self-liberated.

Song 12

Listen son, Prince Dodebum.
I, Marpa the Translator,
Went to the land of India three times.
I attended with devotion the authentic gurus,
Lords Naropa and Maitripa,
And received many tantras, commentaries, and oral instructions.
They granted transmissions of the pith of the four abhishekas.
In particular, I received the ejection and transference of
consciousness.
Not keeping anything secret,
I taught this fully to you, my son.
Do you remember these tantras, commentaries, and oral
instructions, Dodebum?
In general, composite things
Are impermanent and perishable.
Son, this illusory body does not last forever.
Suddenly, the obstacles of Mara have arisen.
The white conch of your skull is broken.
The white silk curtain of your cranial membrane is
torn. Your brain, the divine assembly of the buddhas, has
spilled out. Son, it's quite true that your illusory body is
perishable.

Your venerable father is a mandala of deities.
Draw forth your consciousness through the aperture of Brahma.
Now eject your consciousness into the heart center of your
venerable father.

Song 13

I prostrate to the lord gurus.
To the prajna consort who expounds and understands the
Dharma,
To Dagmema I give this advice.
Steady your mind, not mixing it with the mundane.
Arouse certainty and abandon your grief.
Our son Dodebum, whom we cherished so dearly,
Has passed into the realm of luminosity.
Thus his kindness is equal to the lord guru's.
I will clarify this with these seven reminders of illusion.
There is no one to grieve for.
With impartiality toward sentient beings,
Cherish all beings with kindness, Dagmema.
Dagmema, clear away your grief for our son.
Many sutras and other texts written in gold
And sacred representations of body, speech, and mind
Were produced for the sake of our son Dode.
But Dode has passed into the realm of luminosity.
These sacred representations are ownerless, like a rainbow in the
sky.
With the realisation that appearances are empty,
One cannot find anyone to care for.

However, make offerings to all worthy ones,
Dagmema. O Dagmema, clear away your grief for our son.
The tantras and commentaries obtained through hardship,
The pith oral instructions of the concentrated heart essence,
The quintessence of this gathering of all that is profound,
As well as translation of the literary and colloquial languages
Were all studied for the sake of our son Dode.
But Dode has passed into the realm of luminosity.
Dharma is ownerless, like possessing merely a list of treasures:
With the realisation of Dharmas as equanimity,
O Dagmema, give to all.
O Dagmema, clear away your grief for our son.
Food and wealth gathered through frugality
And cattle and sheep offered by disciples
Were all accumulated for the sake of our son Dode.
But Dode has passed into the realm of luminosity.
Wealth is ownerless, like undiscovered riches underground.
Cattle are ownerless, like wild animals in a meadow.
With the realisation of possessions as mahamudra,
There is no need to tend them.
O Dagmema, give everything away.
O Dagmema, clear away your grief for our son.
Castles and fields in the fatherland of Pesar
And the tower built by Mila
Were all for the sake of our son Dode.
But the castles are ownerless, like a city of gandharvas.
With the realisation of this land as illusory appearance-
emptiness,
Grasping and clinging to it are futile.

O Dagmema, cast off grasping and clinging to castles.
O Dagmema, clear away your grief for our son.
Being polite to relatives of the Mar clan,
But turning our backs to enemies and annoying people
Were done for the sake of our son Dode.
But Dode has passed into the realm of luminosity.
With the realisation that appearance is mind,
There is no difference between friends and enemies.
O Dagmema, meditate on everything as dharmakaya.
O Dagmema, clear away your grief for our son.
In general, it is characteristic of all composite things
That ultimately they are never permanent.
In particular, the connection and relationship
Between ourselves and Tarma Dode have ended.
This is our karma about which nothing can be done.
O Dagmema, do not grieve.
O Dagmema, clear away your grief for our son.
There is nothing other than Dharma for us.
Be kind to those who are impoverished.
We have six sons who remain,
But there is no hope that they will be holders of the teachings.
Nonetheless, cherish them with kindness, as you did Tarma
Dode.
O Dagmema, do not grieve.
O Dagmema, clear away your grief for our son.
In accordance with the prophecy of Mahapandit Naropa,
The lineages of my son-disciples,
Like the waxing moon,
Will grow and spread further and further.

The Kagyu teachings will flourish and expand.
Great benefit for the teachings and beings will be accomplished.
O Dagmema, rejoice and be happy.
O Dagmema, clear away your grief for our son.

Song 14

Lord guru, inseparable from Aksobhya,
Please remain as the crest ornament on the top of my head.
Today, in order to explain the tantras at this feast,
I, the teacher Marpa Chokyi Lodro,
Will sing this useful story.
Hearing of Tsang, I went there.
At the glorious monastery cf Nyugu valley,
Starving for the teachings of the secret mantra,
I waited three years, my mind a hungry ghost.
In general, I thought I wasted my time there.
I thought I would go to Nepal in the South.
Desiring the Dharma, I suffered like a man thirsting for precious
water.
I thought if it ever came about that I knew the Dharma,
I would give it to anyone who desired it.
This Dharma was obtained through hardship, even at the risk of
my life.
I would feel devastated if these profound oral instructions were
to disappear.
Although I have not explained the textual commentaries
To anyone other than Meton and Ngokton,
I told them to explain the Dharma to whomever desires it.

When disciples offered their wealth,
As their guru, I did not restrict my teaching.
And to Great Magician who had no wealth And to Ngokton who
rendered service,
I was neither strict nor loose with the oral instructions.
Therefore, practice the holy Dharma properly.
I obtained these oral instructions through great hardship.
Not wasting my wealth.
I took a hundred and ten measures of gold with me to India.
I made offerings to special shrines.
I made offerings to gurus.
I offered feasts and torma in special places.
The kind service that you sons have rendered
I repay by giving the immeasurable holy Dharma.
With the sustenance of Dharma, practice.
Benefit sentient beings as much as you can.

Song 15

Lord, master of bliss, refuge of beings,
Nirmanakaya, heruka in union with consort,
Possessing the nine moods, within bliss and emptiness
You join in union; coemergent being, I pay homage to you.
By merely witnessing a sign, the meaning is realised.
Whoever truly hears even a corner of this will be liberated.
Not shown by conventional words,
The wisdom of unconditioned truth is bestowed.
At the very moment when movement is blissful,
One is free from suffering.

In this way, since conditioned mind can never be convinced,
In the stream of bliss-emptiness samadhi,
Rest your mind free from thought.
The guru who is like the Buddha has taught this.
Other lineages also say this.
Through an authentic consort,
One's ability becomes developed.
Like a person shooting a bird with an arrow,
One always depends on one's ability.
Even when habitual patterns of desire arise,
This primordially pure mind
Is not corrupted by temporary conditions.
It remains unconditioned, like space.
This is the unpervened natural state.
Free from even a speck of mind's activity,
There is not even a speck to cling to.
Thoroughly trained in the oral instructions,
At the time one leaves this body behind,
One dissolves into the space of paramita.
Thus, mind is unborn.
Mind is like the sky.
Don't corrupt it with a mist of conceptualizations.
The lord Mahapandit Naropa spoke these words:
"In order to practice the Dharma properly,
Like a snake placed in a bamboo tube,
Don't make any effort to move.
Those who suffer from desire
Are like one hit on a sore point.
Don't let your mind of nonaction wander.

The innate nature of mind is primordially empty.
Like smashing things with a hammer,
It liberates through seeing, touching, and thinking."
Please understand this completely.
This is a meditation song of mahamudra.
Since the holy Dharma benefits others,
Don't clutch it in a death grip, Metonpa.
For those who are worthy
Don't keep it secret, but give them instructions.

Song 16

Although everyone has a lineage,
If one has the dakini's lineage, that is it.
Although everyone has forefathers,
If one has Tilopa, that is it.
Although everyone has a guru,
If one has Naropa, that is it.
Although everyone has oral instructions,
If one has the hearing lineage, that is it.
Although everyone attains enlightenment by meditating,
If one becomes enlightened without effort in meditation, that is
it.

Song 17

Why shouldn't my lineage be famed,
Since we possess the Dharma eye of the dakinis.
Why shouldn't the forefathers be famed,

Since Tilopa is no one other than the buddha.
Why shouldn't my guru be famed,
Since Naropa is a torch of Dharma.
Why shouldn't I be famed,
Since I am the only heart son of Naropa.
Why shouldn't the oral instructions be famed,
Since this wish-fulfilling jewel of the hearing lineage
Is the special Dharma that no one else possesses.

Glossary

Abhisheka

In the Tibetan Buddhist tradition, an abhisheka is a method for performing esoteric transmission, a way to offer blessings of a lineage to participants, or it can be also an empowerment to begin a particular meditation practice.

Anuttara-yoga-tantra

A term commonly used to indicate the highest or 'supreme' form of the four classes of tantras and their associated practices according to Tantric Buddhism in Tibet. Historically, they are considered to be the latest to have been developed and compiled in India, possibly between the early 8th and the 11th century, although traditionally they were considered to have been promulgated during the lifetime of Sakyamuni and then concealed until they later re-emerged in the human world. There are three categories of anuttara-yoga-tantras: Father Tantras, Mother Tantras, and Non-dual Tantras. Father Tantras, as typified by the Guhyasamja Tantra, emphasize the so-called generation phase (utpatti-krama) of meditative transformation; the Mother

Tantras, typified by the Hevajra Tantra, the completion phase (sapanna-krama); the Non-dual Tantras, typified by the Kalacakra Tantra, which combines both the generation and the completion phases. Practices associated with many tantras of this class involve sexual yoga, fierce rites of destruction, and hence are treated with great secrecy, to be taught only to those who have received the appropriate initiations or abhisheka.

Bardo

The Tibetan word bardo means literally 'intermediate state' also translated as 'transitional state' or 'in-between state' or 'liminal state'. Used somewhat loosely, the term bardo may refer to the state of existence intermediate between two lives on earth. According to Tibetan tradition, after death and before one's next birth, when one's consciousness is not connected with a physical body, one experiences a variety of phenomena. These usually follow a particular sequence of degeneration from, just after death, the clearest experiences of reality of which one is spiritually capable, to, later on, terrifying hallucinations arising from the impulses of one's previous unskillful actions. For the spiritually advanced the bardo offers a state of great opportunity for liberation, since transcendental insight may arise with the direct experience of reality, while for others it can become a place of danger as the karmically created hallucinations can impel one into a less than desirable rebirth.

Charnel Ground Ornaments and Implements

The Charnel Ground Ornaments can be found in images

depicting dakinis, yoginis, dharmapalas and a few other deities. They are: Crown of five skulls, Bone necklace, Bone armlets, Bone bracelets, Bone skirt and Bone anklets. Apart from these ornaments, deities are shown with several implements made from (mostly human) bones that have been gathered in a charnel ground as well: Bone trumpet, Skull cup and Skull drum.

Dakini

In Vajrayana, it is a designation for the wrathful and semi-wrathful female deities among the yidams. Tibetan texts indicate these deities as females who move on the highest level of reality. Their nudity is said to symbolise the diamond-like clarity of the truth they unveil. A dakini is also defined as the 'feminine energy principle, associated with knowledge and intelligence, which may be either destructive or creative'.

Dharmata

The term denotes what is 'real'; in its widest sense, this includes everything that is, whether or not it is observable or comprehensible. Reality in this sense includes 'being' and sometimes is considered to include 'nothingness' as well. By contrast, the term 'existence' is often restricted solely to being (compare with nature).

Dharampalas

The term is most often used for eight major and several minor guardians of Tantric Buddhism. Dharmapalas can usually be recognized by various attributes they are depicted as wearing or carrying. Among these, one finds clothing made of tiger, elephant or human skin, bone or skull-made anklets, garlands, necklaces or girdles; as well as the crown of five skulls. Hand-held implements include the skull cup and double skull drum as well the flaying knife and many more.

Ganacakra

In the great cultures of the past, the Sumerian, Chaldean, Egyptian, Hellenic, and the Indian, a chief place in the human drama of spiritual devotion belonged to the celebration of sacramental mysteries. From the schools of Tantra in India, a sacramental inheritance, in the form of the ganacakra, reached the Lamaist colleges of Tibet. It is a sacred rite which one approaches in a state of spiritual awe and wonder, seeking within its mystery a gateway to personal transformation. Ganacakra is used as a generic term for various tantric assemblies or feasts, in which practitioners meet to chant mantra, enact mudra, make votive offerings and practice various tantric rituals as part of a sadhana, or spiritual practice. The ganacakra often comprises a sacramental meal and festivities such as dancing.

Guhyasamaja

The Guhyasamaja, or 'Secret Assembly,' Tantra, known as the king of the tantras, was developed at an early date in history to aid the Buddhist practitioner in understanding and practicing Tantric Buddhism to attain enlightenment. It is an esoteric and highly symbolic form of Buddhism, which developed in India and became dominant in Tibet. The Guhyasamaja Tantra, translated in the 8th century A.D., was one of the first Sanskrit works to be translated into Tibetan language. According to the Guhyasamaja-Mahakalparaja, the central deity of the mandala of Akshobhyavajra is Vajradhara, the cosmic consciousness, spotless brightness, which owing to its inner law, must expand into manifold universe, gradually disintegrating in the process, but finally returning to initial unity.

Hevajra

A Buddhist Tantra of twenty chapters, thought to have originated in the eighth century. The name is based on the male deity Hevajra, a personified symbol for the Buddhist concept of a supreme being in the state of nonduality, and as such he is most often depicted or visualised in union (Tib: *yab-yum*) with the goddess Nairatmya. The Hevajra Tantra teaches the Union of Skillful Means and Profound Cognition; and states that such union is helpful in achieving the powers known as siddhis. The text belongs to the higher or Inner Tantras and includes the famous quote explaining a basic tenet of the Tantra in only a few words: "One must rise by that by which one falls. By whatever thing the world is bound, by that the bond is unfastened. Beings are bound by passion and are released by utilising passion."

Jetsun

Jetsun is a Tibetan title meaning 'venerable' or 'reverend'. It is a term applied to revered teachers of Tibetan Buddhism. The title is applied to hermits and learned lamas such as Jetsun Milarepa. Je refers to those of high rank, including kings and nobles; tsun refers to those of noble rank, or those who are monastic, or those who combine the three characteristics of being learned, noble, and good.

Kagyu Lineage

The Kagyu lineage originated with the great yogi Tilopa who lived in Northern India around the 10th century A.D. Tilopa received the four special transmissions (Tib: *bka-babs-bzhi*) and mastered them. The masters associated with each of the four transmissions are: the first of the four came from Nagarjuna and consists of two tantras, the Sangwa Düpa Tantra (Skr: *Guhyasamaja*) and the Denshi Tantra. It also incorporates the practices called 'Illusory Body' (Tib: *sgyu-lus*) and 'Transference' (Tib: *pho-ba*). The second special transmission came from Nakpopa and includes the tantra called Gyuma Chenmo (Skr: *Mahamaya*) and the practice called 'Conscious Dreaming' (Tib: *rmi-lam*). The third special transmission came from Lawapa. It includes the Demchok Tantra and the practice of 'Clear Light' (Tib: *od-gsal*). The fourth was transmitted from Khandro Kalpa Zangmo and includes the tantra known as Gyepa Dorje (Skr: *Hevajra*), and the practice called Tummo. These teachings were passed on from Tilopa to Naropa, and were systematized as the Six Yogas of Naropa, considered a central theme in the Kagyu Lineage. Naropa transmitted his knowledge to Marpa, the great translator who journeyed from Tibet to India in order to receive instructions and who subsequently returned to Tibet and spread the teachings of the Dharma. His student, Milarepa, became one of Tibet's great yogis.

Lotsawa

Lotsawa is a Tibetan word used as a title to refer to the native Tibetan translators, such as Vairotsana, Rinchen Zangpo, Marpa and others, who worked alongside Indian scholars or pundits to translate the texts of the Buddhist canons into Tibetan from Sanskrit, Chinese and other Asian languages. It is thought to derive from the Sanskrit locchava, which is said to mean 'bilingual' or 'eyes of the world.' The term is also used to refer to modern-day translators of Tibetan Buddhist texts

Mahamaya

The Mahamaya-tantra is a tantra associated with Dream Yoga. It is considered by Tibetan Buddhism to be the Mother Tantra. In order to make the time we spend dreaming more meaningful, we must first recognise that we are dreaming. That is the initial exercise. The next step is called transforming the dream; the third is known as multiplying. The fourth practice is to unify the dream with the clear light. Recognising, transforming, multiplying and unifying the dream with the luminosity of the true nature; these four outline the essential applications of dream yoga.

Mahamudra

Mahamudra is most well-known as a teaching within the Kagyu lineages of Tibetan Buddhism. All of the various Tibetan Mahamudra lineages originated with the tantric Mahasiddhas of Pala empire India in the 8th to 12th Centuries. The 'Profound Action' lineage originated with Maitreya and Asanga and was introduced to Tibet by Marpa and Atisha. Marpa introduced the lineage to the Kagyu school and Atisha to the Kadam school, which later produced the Gelug school. Marpa introduced to Tibet the 'Profound Blessing Meditation Experience' lineage that is believed to have originated with the primordial Buddha Vajradhara and was passed to Tilopa and Naropa. Marpa also introduced a Mahamudra lineage that traces back to Saraha and Maitripa. Mahamudra literally means 'great seal' or 'great symbol', an absolute seal, totality, unchangeability. Sealing something implies that you cannot destroy it. The term Mahamudra refers to the realisation arising from certain advanced forms of Buddhist meditation practice, comprising methods of attaining a direct introduction to the nature and essence of the mind. Mahamudra is believed to enable one to realise the mindstream's innate purity, clarity and perfection, known by the term 'buddha nature'.

Paramita

The term Paramita or Parami means 'Perfect' or 'Perfection'. In Buddhism, the Paramitas refer to the perfection or culmination of certain virtues. In Buddhism, these virtues are cultivated as a way of purification, purifying karma and helping the aspirant to live an unobstructed life, while reaching the goal of Enlightenment.

Prajna

Prajna has been translated as 'wisdom', 'understanding', 'discernment', 'cognitive acuity', or 'know-how'. In some sects of Buddhism, it especially refers to the wisdom that is based on the direct realisation of the Four Noble Truths, impermanence, interdependent origination, non-self, emptiness, etc. Prajna is the wisdom that is able to extinguish afflictions and bring about enlightenment.

Prajnaparamita

The Prajnaparamita Sutras are a genre of Mahayana Buddhist scriptures dealing with the subject of the Perfection of Wisdom. The term Prajnaparamita alone never refers to a specific text, but always to the class of literature. The Perfection of Wisdom states that there is no multiplicity: all is one. Even existence (samsara) and nirvana are essentially the same, and both have no inherent nature, but arise from the projections of one's mind. The view of The Perfection of Wisdom is that words and analysis have a practical application in that they are necessary for us to function in this world but, ultimately, all that we experience is a dream painted on a surface with no inherent nature.

Samaya

The samaya is a set of vows or precepts given to initiates of an esoteric Vajrayana Buddhist order as part of the abhisheka ceremony of empowerment or initiation that creates a bond between the guru and disciple.

Six Yogas of Naropa

The Six Yogas of Naropa, also called Naro's Six Doctrines, describe a set of advanced Tibetan Buddhist tantric practice and meditation sadhana compiled in and around the time of the Indian monk and mystic Naropa (1016-1100 AD), and conveyed to his student Marpa the translator. The Six Yogas were intended to help in the attainment of siddhi and enlightenment in an accelerated manner.

They are:

Tummo: the Yoga of Inner Heat (or Mystic heat).
Gyulu: the Yoga of the Illusory Body.
Osel: the Yoga of the Clear Light or Radiant Light.
Milam: the Yoga of the Dream State.
Bardo: the Yoga of the Intermediate State.
Phowa: the Yoga of the Transference of Consciousness, to a pure Buddhafield.

Vajrayana

Vajrayana Buddhism is esoteric, in the sense that the transmission of certain teachings only occurs directly from teacher to student during an initiation or empowerment and cannot be simply learned from a book. The term 'vajra' denoted the thunderbolt, a legendary weapon and divine attribute that was made from an adamantine, or indestructible substance, which could pierce and penetrate any obstacle. So the Vajrayana is sometimes rendered in English as The Adamantine Vehicle or The Diamond Vehicle. Vajrayana Buddhism is also known as Tantric Buddhism, Tantrayana, or Mantrayana. The period of Vajrayana Buddhism has been classified as the fifth or final period of Indian Buddhism. Vajrayana probably came into existence in the 6th or 7th century AD, while the term Vajrayana first came into evidence in the 8th century AD. Its scriptures are called the Tantras. The distinctive feature of Vajrayana Buddhism is ritual, which is used as a substitute or alternative for the earlier abstract meditations.

According to Vajrayana scriptures, it is one of the three routes to enlightenment, the other two being Hinayana and Mahayana.

Yidam

A yidam is the personal deity (male or female) of a practitioner, embodying her or his potential nature, once it is awakened. It is chosen and visualised according to one's psychological makeup. There are six types of yidams, with the defining attributes of a given deity depending on gender and the three qualities defined as gentle, semi-fierce or fierce.

Male: signifies awakened energy, skillful means, and bliss
Female: signifies compassion, emptiness, and profound cognition (or wisdom)
Gentle: stimulates the gentle aspects of a student and awaken his or her openness
Semi-fierce: represents the energy that finds expression in both passion and anger
Fierce: symbolises the dynamic energy of true anger, cutting through all superficial compassion and learned disbelief in oneself and one's intrinsic Buddha-nature.

Yogini

Most often the term is used for one or more goddesses within Buddhism and Tantra. Although the traditional number of these yoginis is said to be 64, various lists give different names and sometimes come to a different number; varying from school to school and from century to century.